The impact of

ATLANTEANS

in the

South and West

David
Toy

© 2011 Venture Publications Ltd

ISBN 978 1905 304 34 9

The only single-deck Atlanteans supplied to an operator in the South and West were twelve delivered to Portsmouth, with Seddon bodies as seen below. (John Senior)

Contents

David Toy was born in Kent in 1946 and in his school days saw Maidstone & District introduce the Leyland Atlantean into their fleet. Having an interest in transport he joined Reed Transport (Reed Paper Group) and trained in heavy vehicle engineering. After qualifying as an engineer he moved into the bus industry in 1971 and started his management career at Reading Transport where he became the Engineering Assistant to the Chief Engineer. At the age of 28 he was appointed Chief Engineer of Brighton Borough Transport where he stayed for eight years before joining the Scottish Bus Group.

He held several positions within the Scottish Bus Group including Chief Engineer of Northern Scottish (including a joint position as Chief Engineer of Grampian Regional Transport), Engineering Manager of SBG Engineering and Chief Engineer of Kelvin and Western/Clydeside Scottish. With the privatisation of the group he became Engineering Director of Western Buses. After the sale to Stagecoach in 1994 he moved to British Bus as Engineering Director of London & Country until its demise. Then onto the Callett Group (Southern National/Devon Red Bus) in the same position at Taunton; the group was eventually sold to First Group. Staying with First he became Engineering Director of First Southern National and then First Hampshire and Dorset.

David retired in 2005 after 31 years in senior management within the industry; the Leyland Atlantean followed him to many of the companies. At Brighton he was responsible for vehicle specification and purchase and introduced many new ideas to the Brighton fleet.

Living now in Seaford, East Sussex, with his wife Barbara he enjoys writing books and magazine articles. Keeping in touch with the industry, he is the Chairman of the local centre of the Institute of Road Transport Engineers.

LEYLAND ATLANTEAN REAR-ENGINED DOUBLE-DECKER

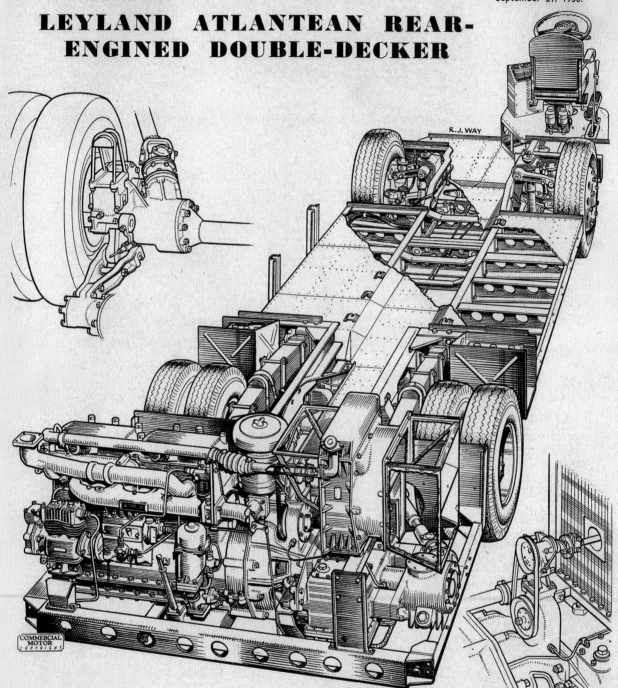

The Leyland Atlantean is a rear-engined semi-integral 78-seat double-decker, the underframing, floor and mechanical components of which are clearly shown in this drawing. The rear engine gives many advantages, not the least of which is the low floor height. This allows both saloons to be of full height, whilst the overall laden height of the bus is kept down to 13 ft. 2¾ in.

A Leyland 0.600 oil engine powers the Atlantean. This six-cylindered unit develops 125 b.h.p. at 1,800 r.p.m. and is used in conjunction with a centrifugal single-plate clutch and semi-automatic epicyclic gearbox. This gearbox has four forward ratios, and can be provided as a fully automatic version. The drive is taken at an angle of 72° into the back of the spiral-bevel and helical-spur-gear double-reduction rear axle.

The rear axle and the parallel-link forming part of the off-side rear suspension are seen in the inset sketch (top, left). The rear spring is not shown, but this is pivoted on rubber bushes to the top of the axle case. The leaf spring and the trailing link on each side of the axle form a Watts linkage which ensures almost vertical movement of the axle at all stages of spring deflection.

Torsion bars and double wishbones constitute the front suspension, with telescopic dampers. A dual air-hydraulic braking system is used: this has independent hydraulic circuits to the front and rear axles, with two air-hydraulic actuators controlled by a single pedal valve.

A system of heating and ventilation, using the engine radiator and fan, has been devised which eliminates the need for opening windows in the body. The fan-drive layout is shown in the lower sketch: it consists of a V-belt driven from a train of gears at the front of the gearbox. The unladen weight of the Atlantean is 7¾ tons, and it is built to body dimensions of 30 ft. by 8 ft. (Stand 85).

Introduction

The Leyland Atlantean production was longer than any other rear-engine double-deck bus, the first deliveries were in 1958 and the last in 1984, a total of 26 years. Within the south and west, the Leyland Atlantean did not disappear from service until the early 21st century, when it was still in use with two operators whose history went back to the original purchaser. Unlike its competitors, it stayed with the same in-house Leyland engine (O.600 or the O.680) and chassis layout, the only changes were the short production of the drop-centre axle variant, PDR1/2 and PDR1/3. It was the first rear-engined double-decker to reach full production and other manufacturers were to follow in the forthcoming years. At first, the early buses had reliability problems, but as time went on the chassis was updated with various changes to its specification and when the AN68 version was launched in 1972, it became a well-respected and reliable bus in service.

Over the years, the majority of the major bus operators in the south and west used the Leyland Atlantean; these included both company (BET) and municipal fleets. Most were already loyal to Leyland with the PD2 and PD3 range, but others had been AEC or Guy customers and changed their allegiance as the Atlantean production grew. A small number fell into the Transport Holding Company fleets, when the original owner was purchased by a subsidiary company, very much a contrast to the standard Bristol KSW or Lodekka, which the group had to purchase. Two operators stayed loyal to the Atlantean and continued to purchase the model throughout its production life, those being Plymouth and Southampton. Others such as Maidstone & District and Bournemouth did not put all their eggs in one basket and purchased the Daimler Fleetline as well as the Atlantean. Devon General made a return to the front engine chassis due to the unreliability of the early Leyland Atlanteans.

With its high seating capacity it was a vehicle that would be ideal for trolleybus replacement, and Maidstone & District at Hastings, Bournemouth, Maidstone and Portsmouth municipals all used the Atlantean to remove the problems of the inflexibility of the overhead. With a larger seating capacity, it was predicted that the number of buses on a route could be reduced and help to improve operational costs. In the early years, Leyland introduced a marketing campaign for the Leyland Atlantean with various advertising slogans and gained a high number of orders throughout the country. The following is the history of the Atlantean days in the south and west and its competitors, with an insight into the engineering and development of the bus.

Opposite: A sectioned drawing of the new concept in double-deck bus design which appeared in The Commercial Motor in September 1956. (Commercial Motor)

1 : The Beginning

In the early 1950s, all double-deckers were front-engined and the majority had a rear entrance. There was a wide choice of both chassis and body manufacturers with Leyland, AEC, Daimler and Guy being in the forefront of production numbers. The British Transport Commission companies were tied into the Bristol chassis with Eastern Coach Works bodies. In the south and west there had been a cross section of allegiance to manufacturers with Devon General, East Kent, Southampton Corporation and Southdown purchasing Guy. Plymouth and Portsmouth municipals had been Leyland customers; Southdown had a dual supply and purchased from Leyland and Guy. Maidstone & District had built up a large Bristol K6A fleet, and when they were not available turned first to Leyland with the PD2 and then to the AEC Regent V. Brighton and Eastbourne Corporations, not large purchasers, had stayed with AEC. London had split their orders between AEC and Leyland and was developing the Routemaster. Things were to change as Leyland with the PD2 and AEC with the Regent V would soon take the lead.

In 1952, Leyland started to build a rear-engined chassis that would set the trend for the industry in the coming years. It had a Leyland O.350 lightly turbocharged engine mounted transversely at the rear, producing 115 bhp at 2,200 rpm. Having a rear entrance the larger 9.8 litre O.600 engine could not be fitted due to the Construction and Use regulations requiring an 18in cutback at the entrance for an emergency exit. The gearbox was a Wilson pre-selective unit with a centrifugal clutch and the drive was angled to a dropped-centre rear axle. Unlike the current practice of the time of having a separate chassis, it had a semi-integral underframe with independent front suspension and coil and leaf at the rear. Leyland used Saunders-Roe to body the underframe which at the time seemed an unusual choice as they had their own body building capabilities – but, as we now know, not for much longer. The body had a full width cab, not unlike a trolleybus, and seated 61 with an overall height of 13ft 3in giving a full height in both saloons. The bus was a lightweight vehicle with an unladen weight of 6.89 tons.

In 1954, it was demonstrated to the industry and was operated in service by several of the BET companies in the south and west, namely Devon General, Southdown and Maidstone & District. It was shown to obtain the views from the industry of a rear-engine layout. The Construction & Use regulations changed in June 1956 to allow a permitted length of 30ft on two axles, and the overall weight limit was increased to 14 tons. In the light of this Leyland was quick to introduce the PD3 Titan range at the new length.

The time was now right for a complete rethink of the whole rear-engined bus idea and, accordingly, a fresh design team under the leadership of Dr Mueller, who had joined Leyland in 1947 from Germany, took a new look at the concept to include the revised length and would now use Metro-Cammell-Weymann as the partner for

Leyland's Lowloader on demonstration with Southdown in 1954. It had a rear entrance with a turbocharged Leyland O.350 engine fitted transversely also at the rear. (Southdown Enthusiasts Club)

the body, another sign of things to come. At 30ft, the axle could be set back with a front entrance under control of the driver, and have a high seating capacity. The engine would be at the rear and the Leyland 9.8-litre O.600 engine could be fitted transversely, coupled to a pneumocyclic gearbox with an angle drive to the rear axle. There was no conventional chassis as in the Leyland PD Titan range; it was made of channel sections with light alloy plates laid on top as clearly shown in the full-page frontispiece on page 6. These plates would be used for the bodybuilder to attach the floor. Independent front suspension was fitted with reverse camber springs and rubber-mounted trailing links on the rear. The brakes were two-line air over hydraulic, again a change from the norm for a Leyland double-decker. The brakes were operated by two air cylinders attached to hydraulic master cylinders which then passed brake fluid to the wheel cylinders to operate the brakes. The axle had a dropped centre with the differential positioned to the right hand side; this would give a low gangway and low overall height.

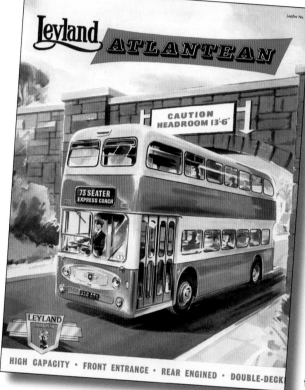

The pneumocyclic gearbox was not in common use, as most double-deck vehicles produced by Leyland had a manual gearbox with a conventional clutch pedal. The electrically-operated clutch was activated by a small switch attached to the steering column. This operated air pistons, which clamped the epicyclic gear train and engaged the relevant gear. A centrifugal clutch was used to take up the drive between the engine and gearbox, thus removing the need for a clutch pedal and this comprised of six pivoted weights which engaged the clutch at 500rpm. All of this was aimed to make life easier for the driver and for the engineering department. The engine and gearbox was on a detachable subframe and had to be removed as one unit. The radiator was also at the rear, positioned above the gearbox. Access to the engine bay was by two hinged doors and this gave better accessibility than a front engine double-decker.

The body was integral to the chassis; Leyland had produced single-deck vehicles with MCW in the past but this was a first on a double-deck. The wheelbase was 16ft 3in and by using the dropped centre-axle, a low height of 13ft 3in was achieved. This allowed conventional seating in both saloons, unlike the current lowbridge vehicles of the time with bench seats on the upper-deck. At 30ft, it gave a total seating of 78 with five standing and this was a higher capacity than the same length PD3. With all the weight at the back, MCW increased the pillar sections and had a strengthened section within the lower saloon by the rear wheel arches. The body style was very square with the engine compartment built into the body and it had a novel heating and ventilating system with no opening side windows, though there were two small opening windows in the front upper-deck.

The prototype Atlantean quickly found itself used in Leyland promotional material and the low height was strongly promoted along with the front entrance and rear engine. (Leyland)

The prototype integral Leyland Atlantean, 281 ATC, was the star of the 1956 Commercial Motor Show where it stood out against all other double-deckers. It was the trendsetter of bus design, with its rear engine layout. (Hustwitt collection)

The Leyland Atlantean was the star of the 1956 *Commercial Motor Show* and Leyland played on the passenger safety with the front entrance under the control of the driver whilst also having a higher seating capacity than current buses. However, with costs becoming a problem for operators, they did not want to hear that this new model would cost 40% more than a conventional double-deck bus. The industry had not been in favour of the fully integral vehicle, and various parts of the new Atlantean were also untried. Nevertheless, an overall weight of 7.8 tons was very impressive for a rear-engine bus at any date, and today's designers of double-deck vehicles must wonder how this has now increased to 12 tons?

The new vehicle was registered 281 ATC and was demonstrated to various companies, mainly in the BET Group. Leyland gained operators comments and realised that the integral format and the complex dropped axle were a burden to the cost of the project. They also used this vehicle to alter the engine bay, after complaints of the noise level at the rear, to what was to become the standard Atlantean rear end with a bustle. A second vehicle was built as a test bed, and after extensive testing Leyland came upon problems with cracks within the underframe and the decision was made to revamp the vehicle. Leyland knew that the front entrance layout with a rear-engine was the way to proceed but taking on board the comments of operators, and the problems found on the test vehicle, the design team revised the vehicle to make it more acceptable to the industry. In early September 1958 the new Atlantean was introduced to the trade press, with complete vehicles to be shown at the forthcoming *Commercial Motor Show* at Earls Court.

There was to be no pre-production chassis, Leyland made the decision to proceed into full production, a brave decision or a recipe for disaster? We shall shortly see.

Leyland started to advertise the Atlantean in the trade magazines; this is the advertisement in the 1958 show edition of the *Bus and Coach* magazine. The drawing clearly shows how Leyland achieved the lowbridge layout with bench seats at the rear of the upper deck. (Bus and Coach)

Taken from the 1956 Leyland Atlantean brochure, the design of the underframe can be clearly seen with the front independent suspension. The floor of the body was laid on top of Leyland's own sections. A detailed view of the suspension is shown below and was very advanced for its day; it did not reappear on a production Leyland double-decker until the Titan in the mid-1970s. (Leyland)

FABRICATED FRAME OF GREAT STRENGTH AND LIGHTNESS

The frame is constructed from two alloy-steel longitudinal members of channel section 8.5 in. deep with 3 in. flanges and ⅜ in. thick. To these are bolted the crossmembers and outriggers, arranged to give the effect of continuous transverse beams. Floor plates of light alloy are directly rivetted to the channels and form a top connection between crossmembers and outriggers to reinforce the structure without adding excessive weight. The mid and rear section outriggers are braced at their extremities by longitudinal members.
As the vehicle is of semi-integral construction with the body pillars permanently connected to the chassis outriggers, the body assists the frame to carry the full load, although the chassis itself is sufficiently strong to run under its own power.

This semi-integral design has the outstanding advantages of high rigidity with low weight, and a free choice of body layout.

The power unit of the Atlantean develops 125 b.h.p. and a torque as high as 410 lb. ft., and has gained an unrivalled world-wide reputation for efficiency, economy and long life.

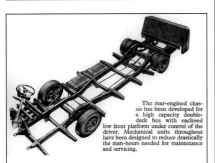

The rear-engined chassis has been developed for a high capacity double-deck bus with enclosed low front platform under control of the driver. Mechanical units throughout have been designed to reduce drastically the man-hours needed for maintenance and servicing.

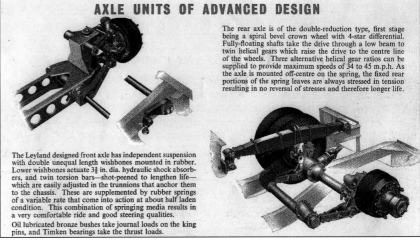

AXLE UNITS OF ADVANCED DESIGN

The rear axle is of the double-reduction type, first stage being a spiral bevel crown wheel with 4-star differential. Fully-floating shafts take the drive through a low beam to twin helical gears which raise the drive to the centre line of the wheels. Three alternative helical gear ratios can be supplied to provide maximum speeds of 34 to 45 m.p.h. As the axle is mounted off-centre on the spring, the fixed rear portions of the spring leaves are always stressed in tension resulting in no reversal of stresses and therefore longer life.

The Leyland designed front axle has independent suspension with double unequal length wishbones mounted in rubber. Lower wishbones actuate 3⅝ in. dia. hydraulic shock absorbers, and twin torsion bars—shot-peened to lengthen life—which are easily adjusted in the trunnions that anchor them to the chassis. These are supplemented by rubber springs of a variable rate that come into action at about half laden condition. This combination of springing media results in a very comfortable ride and good steering qualities.
Oil lubricated bronze bushes take journal loads on the king pins, and Timken bearings take the thrust loads.

Into Production

The revised Atlantean had a separate chassis with bolted outriggers for the body attachment. This would give the industry a choice of body supplier, which was the normal practice with a front-engined double-decker. The engine and transmission was encased in a bustle at the rear. Leyland kept the O.600 engine rated at 125bhp at 1,800rpm with a pneumocyclic gearbox, and this was mounted on a bolted subframe attached to the chassis. Gone was the independent front suspension and air over hydraulic brakes, Leyland had gone back to conventional road springs with a beam front axle and a full single line air braking system. A straight axle had replaced the dropped centre unit and Leyland offered the bodybuilders two alternative heights. The overall price had been reduced and the new Atlantean was a more efficient vehicle to produce but at around £7,000 for a complete bus the price was still higher than a front-engined PD3 and its competitors. Leyland kept the original name of Atlantean with the code of PDR1/1 (Passenger Double-deck Rear-engine) and produced it with a wheelbase of 16ft 3in, giving an overall length of 30ft and 8ft width. Changing the rear axle to a conventional unit raised the floor height by 1ft, losing its equal height in both saloons. Leyland offered a guarantee on the chassis of twelve months or until 40,000 miles had been covered, whichever came first.

The rear-engined concept, in theory, should have made the front-engined bus obsolete overnight but it was going to be many years before the last Leyland PD3 and AEC Regent V examples came off the production lines. Some operators stayed away until the rear-engined bus had become more reliable. With a rear-engined chassis, engineering costs would never be the same as its front-engined counterpart, they were always going to increase.

The engine and transmission on the Atlantean was fitted onto a subframe with the radiator sitting on top of the gearbox and Leyland carried out demonstrations to show how quickly the powerpack could be removed and replaced from the chassis. The Leyland O.600 engine had proved to be very reliable in the PD2 and PD3 range, but sadly it was not going to be the same with the early Atlantean.

The standard full height bus measured 14ft 6in and would seat up to 78 passengers, with the lead body builder MCW; a lowbridge version was built to a height of 13ft 4in. This was achieved by raising the rear floor over the rear axle, and having a sunken gangway by the last four rows of seats on the upper-deck. These were bench seats, the same as a conventional lowbridge double-decker, and the maximum seating was reduced to 73.

MCW had three bodied examples at the 1958 *Commercial Motor Show*. Maidstone & District had DL43 (43 DKT) the first of 14 lowbridge examples for its fleet – the body was built at the Weymann factory at Addlestone in Surrey. The first MCW-designed body for the Atlantean was very square and upright and was of steel construction attached to the chassis by the crossmembers. Doors were of the jack-knife type and were under the direct control of the driver; it had a rearward ascending staircase with a luggage pen and a small locker for the conductor. The seats on the Maidstone & District vehicle were in a green moquette and leather with the ceiling covered in cream Darvic; the lower internal panels were also green. Internal lighting was by 14 conventional bulbs in each saloon with a single bulb over the entrance door. The bell was operated by a continuous strip attached to the ceiling. Maidstone & District had one of the better liveries, being dark green and cream and, with the M&D cream bib below the front windscreens, this helped to enhance the vehicle's appearance.

The other MCW-bodied Atlanteans to be seen at the show were for Wallasey Corporation (highbridge) No. 1 (FHF 451) and for BET subsidiary J James (lowbridge) No. 227 (RTH 637); there was also an Alexander-bodied vehicle for Glasgow Corporation LA1 (FYS 998). Orders were announced at the show from the BET Group for a number of their companies including 50 for Maidstone & District and 17 for Devon General with a further 23 to follow. They were to have MCW Group bodies; all of Devon General's were highbridge and 14 of Maidstone & District were to be lowbridge, the same as the show model DL43. A number of the Maidstone Atlanteans were to be based in the Hastings area as replacements for the trolleybus system. The last two of the order had coach seating, an unusual choice for Maidstone & District for a double-decker. An order had been placed by the first independent operator for the Atlantean, Shergold and White of Salisbury (Silver Star). They had been a loyal customer of Leyland and operated local services as well as contracts with the army at the local garrison. The other large double-deck order for the south and west was for 40 AEC Regent Vs with Park Royal front-entrance bodies for East Kent; one of these was also exhibited at the show.

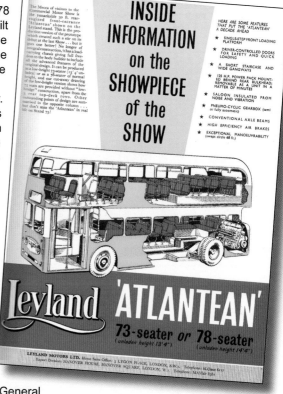

The finished product; the first Metro-Cammell-bodied Leyland Atlantean PDR1/1 to enter service was Wallasey Corporation's No. 1 (FHF 451) in December 1958. Fittingly, it survives in preservation. (David Toy)

Facing page: If driving the Atlantean was child's play and changing the entire engine could be done in under 25 minutes, what could possibly go wrong with this new bus. What indeed? (STA)

This series of photographs shows the powerpack change carried out in a very controlled test on a Leyland Atlantean. The manufacturer stated that a customer could have a spare unit ready for changing, and whilst this might be viable for the larger operator, the cost to a smaller one would be very high; large operators would have needed to think carefully as the frequent early failures of engines and gearboxes meant a large float of units would have been required. The test vehicle was 398 JTB, Leyland's first demonstrator fitted with a Metro-Cammell 77-seat body. The powerpack was removed and refitted in 24mins 15sec. (Colin Curtis collection)

The soon-to-be familiar 'face' of the Atlantean. (John Senior)

DRIVING AN ATLANTEAN IS CHILD'S PLAY

LEYLAND ATLANTEAN

EASY GEAR CHANGE...LIGHT STEERING...LEYLAND DIESEL POWER
Cuts driver fatigue—speeds journey time

The Atlantean is built to make light work of heavy urban traffic. Consider the facts: full or semi-automatic Pneumo-Cyclic gearbox with 2-pedal control; ultra-easy steering; 68ft swept turning circle gives great manoeuvrability; 0.000 130 bhp Leyland Diesel gives extra power for full loads and steep hills. No wonder the Leyland Atlantean is the most popular rear-engined double decker in the world with over 1,500 now in service.

MORE LEYLAND BUSES AT WORK THAN EVER
In 1964 a new post-war peak in municipally owned Leyland buses was reached; Leylands in municipal service increased by 4.92% and now, over 75% of British bus operating municipalities run Leylands.

LEYLAND MOTORS LIMITED
Head Office & Home Sales: Leyland, Lancs. Telephone: Leyland 21400 and 21661
OVERSEAS SALES: BERKELEY SQUARE HOUSE, BERKELEY SQUARE, LONDON, W.1. Tel: GROsvenor 6050

BUS & COACH. April 1965.

Into Service

The first Atlanteans to enter service in the south and west were with the Maidstone & District fleet in May 1959. All the lowbridge vehicles DL43-57 (DKT 43-57) were allocated to the Hastings area, 23 of the highbridge vehicles were also placed there for the Hastings trolleybus replacement scheme. The others were spread to Maidstone, Gravesend and Tunbridge Wells' garages. Maidstone & District had reached an agreement with the local authority to replace the trolleybuses and then had to have a Statutory Order from Parliament to carry out the changes, trolleybuses, like trams, being subject to Parliamentary approval. The final operation of the Hastings trolleybus system was on the 31st May 1959 after which the new fleet of Atlanteans took over. Maidstone and District had two Atlanteans with different engine specifications: DH493 had the larger O.680 engine and DH497 had the O.600 power plus engine rated at 150bhp. The last two vehicles delivered in October 1959, DH524/5 (524/5 DKT), had 60 coach seats. Although being a Leyland user in its double-deck and coach fleet, Maidstone & District's last double-deck and single-deck order had been with AEC. In 1956, 14 AEC Regent V MD3RV with Park Royal 56-seat bodies fitted with platform doors had entered service, DH476-89 (VKR 476-89). At the same time, eight lowbridge examples with the same chassis and body combination were delivered. There were also a large number of Bristol K6As from the early 'fifties with Saunders bodies that were in need of replacement, as well as Daimler CWG6 and early Guy Arabs.

The first independent operator to take delivery of an Atlantean was, as mentioned, Silver Star in June 1959 with a 73-seat lowbridge body by Weymann. As with its predecessors, it had a star emblem on the upper-deck dome. Devon General started to take delivery of its 17 vehicles in June 1959, DL872-88 (872-88 ATA). These were all highbridge, seating 78, with the standard Metro-Cammell body. They were split between Torquay, Brixham and Kingsteignton depots; cascading of buses took place between depots and at the bottom of the pile Guy Arabs were withdrawn. After a short time in service, the Devon General vehicles were down-seated by two and a luggage pen was fitted.

MCW had an advantage over other bodybuilders as they had gained experience with the 1956 prototype, 281 ATC, and its unregistered sister on stress at the rear of a rear-engined chassis. If the design at the rear was not adequate it would lead to stress cracking and body failure, which would make any operator unhappy.

Both Devon General and Maidstone & District placed further orders for the following year's delivery. The first southern municipality to place an order was Plymouth, for 26 with Metro-Cammell bodies for 1960/61. Plymouth had been a

Silver Star received their first Atlantean, No. 35 (TMW 853), in June 1959 which had a 73-seat lowbridge body by Weymann. When the company was sold to Wilts & Dorset in 1963 No. 35 moved again to the Bristol Omnibus Company and became No. 7997 in that fleet. (See photo on page 28 of a similar vehicle) (John Senior)

loyal customer of Leyland taking batches of PD2 and PD3 chassis over the previous years. Devon General changed their body supplier to Roe for their next batch; Maidstone and District stayed with their same body manufacturer.

Maidstone & District DH523 (523 DKT) was loaned to sister company East Kent from 1st to the 14th September 1959 and was put in service in the Thanet area. East Kent had just taken 40 AEC Regent Vs with an upright full front Park Royal body. After testing the Atlantean they stayed with AEC and ordered further Regent Vs. The two 60-seat coach Atlanteans for Maidstone & District entered service in late 1959 but were never used to their full potential. They ended up on the Isle of Sheppey at Sheerness and were used mainly on bus duties. Surely they were suitable for the longer stage services, Maidstone to Hastings, and the high volume express services? Leyland put two demonstrators in the field and 398 JTB, a standard Metro-Cammell highbridge version seen in the timed engine-change demonstration illustrations, was tried by Plymouth between 22nd and 31st May 1959; it was in a livery similar to that of Maidstone & District.

Leyland did not put any seed vehicles into service before full production

Maidstone & District (a BET subsidiary) operated 46 trolleybuses in the Hastings and Bexhill area and they were replaced with 37 Leyland Atlanteans, the first of which, a highbridge model, is shown below right and which had increased the vehicle seating capacity from 56 to 78 per bus. There were two main trolleybus chassis, the AEC 661T and the Sunbeam W, one of the latter being shown at the Fish Market. The lower view shows Guy BTX trolleybus dating from 1928 overtaking a lowbridge version of the Atlantean, 14 of which were delivered to M&D in 1959, these seating only 73, of course. (RNH/STA)

Maidstone & District's show vehicle was DL43 (43 DKT), a PDR1/1 Leyland Atlantean with a Weymann 73-seat body, seen after being delivered to the company. It had not yet entered service and is standing under the Hastings trolleybus wires. (David Toy)

The last double-deckers purchased by Maidstone & District before the Leyland Atlanteans were AEC Regent Vs, seen below. All had Park Royal bodies with a mixture of low and highbridge bodies and one of the highbridge vehicles, DH489 (VKR 481), is seen on its way to Crowhurst. (M&D and East Kent Bus Club)

The entrance of Maidstone & District's DL43, showing the rear ascending staircase. Within time the front entrance would be the norm for all double-deck buses. (STA)

The upper deck looking forward on Maidstone & District's lowbridge DL43; the sunken gangway can be clearly seen on the left of the rearmost four seats. (STA)

Maidstone & District Leyland Atlantean PDR1/1 DH525 (525 DKT) was one of two of the first batch delivered with 60 coach seats and luggage pens in 1959. The bodies were built by Metro-Cammell and then sent to Weymann for finishing as a coach. Based at Tunbridge Wells and Sheerness depots, they were never used to their full potential as coaches on the longer stage services or regular express operation. DH525 was later converted back as a standard bus with 78 seats in 1966. (MD Woods)

Southdown had been a loyal Leyland customer with the PD2 and in 1958 purchased its first Leyland PD3/4s. They had Northern Counties full-front bodies, seating 69. Over the next eight years Southdown would purchase 285 and all would have Northern Counties bodies. On its way to Brighton is No. 853 (XUF 853) which was delivered in 1960. (Southdown Enthusiasts Club)

Devon General took their first Leyland Atlantean PDR1/1 in June 1959 with Metro-Cammell bodies. The specification included an opening windscreen for the driver but this was changed to a conventional unit early in the vehicles life. On delivery the seating was the standard 78, this was later reduced by two in order to fit a luggage pen. On layover is DL886 (886 ATA) seen on a bright summer's day. The early Atlantean was not a trouble-free vehicle and Devon General returned to the AEC Regent V after taking several batches of Atlanteans.
(David Toy collection)

The 1960 Devon General order for 20 Leyland Atlantean PDR1/1 chassis had a change of body supplier when they turned to Roe, by then part of the ACV group. The Roe body had several problems with its structure which led to an early rebuild due to water ingress, and this led eventually to serious corrosion within the body. Seen left in its original livery is DL901 (901 DTT) from this batch. (David Toy)

Devon General's next delivery in 1961 was seven Roe-bodied Leyland Atlantean PDR1/1s DL918-24 (918-24 GTA) and nine convertible open-top Atlanteans with Metro-Cammell 75-seat bodies 925-33 (925-33 GTA). These had a reverse livery and were all named after local 'Sea Dogs' as listed below.

DL925 Admiral Blake
DL926 Sir Francis Drake
DL927 Sir Martin Frobisher
DL928 Sir Humphrey Gilbert
DL929 Sir Richard Grenville
DL930 Sir John Hawkins
DL931 Sir Thomas Howard
DL932 Earl Howe
DL933 Sir Walter Raleigh

SAFELY ON-
SPEEDILY OFF

LEYLAND ATLANTEAN

THE SOLUTION TO INCREASING PROBLEMS
OF ECONOMICAL CITY TRANSPORT

Designed for a wide entrance door with low step (10 in. kerb height) to facilitate quick, easy passenger entry and exit even during peak hours. The new dropped axle version of the Atlantean gives level floor on both decks and reduces the overall height of the vehicle to 13 ft. 4 in. Powered by the famous 130 b.h.p. Leyland O.600 diesel, the 78-seater Atlantean has quick acceleration and fast schedule capabilities coupled with all round mechanical quietness from its rear mounted engine . . . no wonder more Leylands than ever are in municipal service.

LEYLAND MOTORS LIMITED
Head Office & Home Sales: Leyland, Lancs. Tel: Leyland 21400 & 21601

BUS & COACH, July 1965

When Plymouth came to replace its large fleet of Leyland Titans it chose the Atlantean and the manufacturer was not slow to incorporate these vehicles into its publicity material. (STA)

to help to try to eliminate any early difficulties. Thus when problems did occur, the situation was compounded by the number of chassis that operators had in service. Early problems were with the high rate of failure of the Armstrong front shock absorbers and road springs. Then, despite awareness of the dangers at the design stage, the rear sub-frame began to crack and a flitch plate was added to strengthen the area. To add to the woes the Leyland O.600 engine had lived quite happily at the front in the Titan range, but at the rear things were not the same. The environment was different with higher under-bonnet temperatures at the rear, and any coolant loss or oil not noticed by the driver could cause a major problem with either the engine or gearbox. And the driver was 30ft away in his separate world.

On the PDR1/1, as previously stated, the engine and gearbox were designed to be removed as one unit and a spare replacement fitted. Not all companies could afford this and how many do you hold? The electro-pneumatic valve (which controlled the gears) was fitted on the cylinder block, but this was not in a cool area and when the fan drive shaft broke away it took this valve with it. Leyland modified the fan shaft and the main propeller shaft, which also had a high failure rate. Today we have oils that can be used in various transmissions and are multi purpose but the early Atlantean had different oils for the gearbox and angle drive, and when the seal failed between them the units became contaminated and damage ensued. The whole engine and transmission pack would have to be removed for repairs.

Another problem where the unit had to be removed was the replacement of the centrifugal clutch, which developed a high rate of wear – the vehicle would rattle from the rear end when excessive wear on the weights had occurred. Leyland offered a fluid flywheel drive as a modification, but drivers had to be retrained to pause when changing gear in order to stop the slipping of the bands within the gearbox.

It was becoming apparent that a rear-engined bus is a very good vacuum cleaner and the engine bay would soon have a build-up of road dirt. If there were any oil leaks it would not help the cleanliness of the area as dirt would stick to any oil. This was another cause of high temperatures within the engine bay.

All-in-all the Atlantean was a vehicle well-liked by the traffic department, with its extra seating, but it was turning the engineer's hair grey with its many problems.

This shows the early standard Plymouth PDR1/1 Atlantean with a Metro-Cammell 77-seat body. Number 139 (UDR 339) was the first of the second batch, delivered in 1961. (David Toy)

2 : Atlantean Faces Competition

Guy Wulfrunian

Many operators were unhappy with the rear-engined concept but were attracted by the higher seating capacities the Atlantean offered. In October 1959, Guy Motors announced their new chassis: the Wulfrunian. This offered a front engine, along with the layout of a rear-engined vehicle. The West Riding Automobile Company in Yorkshire had played a major part in its design. The vehicle had various engine options but the Gardner 6LX would be the only one used. Suspension was full air on both axles, a new feature for the industry as well as disc brakes all round, which had an air hydraulic operation. The handbrake was linked to the transmission: this had been common in the truck industry. Another new item was the independent front suspension. Today all modern vehicles have air suspension, disc brakes and independent front suspension but this was all new in 1959. With a front engine the drivers cab was cramped and the staircase was on the nearside. Roe of Leeds built the prototype body, seating 77. The main Guy users in the area tried the demonstrator but no orders were placed. In August 1960, both East Kent and Southdown (who tried it on the coast route 12 between Brighton and Eastbourne) put the Wulfrunian in service. A month later Southampton, who had a large fleet of Guy Arab IIIs, tried the vehicle but took Leyland PD2/27s with Park Royal bodies for their 1961 delivery.

The Wulfrunian design was too advanced for its years and could be described as a 'box of tricks'. Virtually the only orders came from the West Riding Company. Fifteen years later the concept was successfully re-addressed as described on page 64.

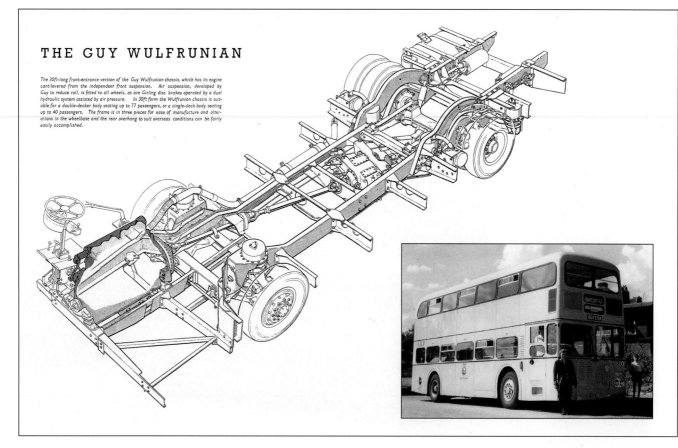

THE GUY WULFRUNIAN

The 30ft-long front-entrance version of the Guy Wulfrunian chassis, which has its engine cantilevered from the independent front suspension. Air suspension, developed by Guy to reduce roll, is fitted to all wheels, as are Girling disc brakes operated by a dual hydraulic system assisted by air pressure. In 30ft form the Wulfrunian chassis is suitable for a double-decker body seating up to 77 passengers, or a single-deck body seating up to 40 passengers. The frame is in three pieces for ease of manufacture and alterations in the wheelbase and the rear overhang to suit overseas conditions can be fairly easily accomplished.

The nearside staircase location is evident in this three-quarter view of a preserved Wulfrunian, whilst the detail shot taken through the open door clearly shows the position of the Gardner 6LX engine on the platform, and the lightweight casing which covered it. (John Senior, both)

Facing page: Taken from the October 1959 edition of *Bus and Coach* magazine is a drawing of the Guy Wulfrunian showing a completely different layout from the Atlantean. The Gardner 6LX engine is at the front with the gearbox placed near the rear and with a dropped centre axle. The air suspension units can be seen quite clearly. Two demonstrators were built with Roe bodies, and almost all production vehicles were bodied by the same manufacturer. This was a bus that went too far on design, and had a short life with its owners due to it having too much new technology too soon. (Bus and Coach)

Facing page, inset: Seen in August 1960, the conductress is standing in front of her new charge – Guy Wulfrunian demonstrator 8072 DA which had a Roe 72-seat body and must have stood out amongst East Kent vehicles, being in an all over yellow livery. Although East Kent had been very loyal to Guy, no orders were placed and they stayed with the AEC Regent/Park Royal combination. (M&D and East Kent Bus Club)

Daimler Fleetline

The main competitor for the Atlantean was launched at the 1960 Commercial Motor Show, namely the Daimler Fleetline. This chassis was offering a Gardner engine, and had a dropped centre axle which meant that the saloon heights could be higher and did not require a sunken gangway as with a lowbridge Leyland Atlantean. Unlike the Atlantean, the engine and gearbox were not close-coupled with the fluid flywheel exposed – there was a rubber coupling between the flywheel and the gearbox. A flat gangway could now be achieved with an overall height of 13ft 4in and so this chassis made the low-height Atlantean obsolete overnight. Leyland now had to look at their product to achieve a similar layout for a low height chassis.

The Daimler Fleetline had standard drum air brakes, the same as the Atlantean, but was now going to open up the market to operators who favoured the Gardner engine – which had a better fuel economy than the Leyland O.600 – and both the 6LW and 6LX would be offered.

Leyland now had to overcome the engineering problems with the Atlanteans that were in service as there was soon to be a direct competitor to its chassis. The Atlantean and the Fleetline both had the same wheelbase which meant that body builders had very little to do in design changes for the new chassis.

Brighton Hove & District was merged with Southdown on 1st January 1969, and the red and cream livery was kept for a few years before the vehicles were all painted into Southdown green. In 1970 ten Gardner-engined Daimler Fleetlines with Northern Counties bodies entered service on local Brighton services. Number 2104 (PUF 204H), is in its original livery whilst behind it is one of Brighton Corporation's Leyland Titans in the later blue livery. (STA).

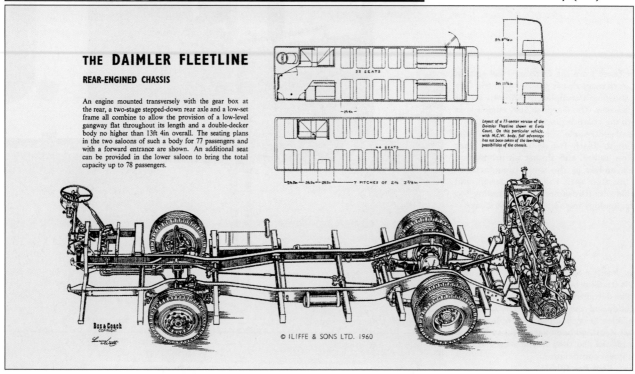

THE DAIMLER FLEETLINE
REAR-ENGINED CHASSIS

An engine mounted transversely with the gear box at the rear, a two-stage stepped-down rear axle and a low-set frame all combine to allow the provision of a low-level gangway flat throughout its length and a double-decker body no higher than 13ft 4in overall. The seating plans in the two saloons of such a body for 77 passengers and with a forward entrance are shown. An additional seat can be provided in the lower saloon to bring the total capacity up to 78 passengers.

Layout of a 77-seater version of the Daimler Fleetline shown at Earls Court. On this particular vehicle, with M.C.W. body, full advantage has not been taken of the low-height possibilities of the chassis.

© ILIFFE & SONS LTD. 1960

The improvement in body design can be seen on Bournemouth's Daimler Fleetline No. 194 (CRU 194C) with a revised Weymann body. This batch had distinctive Alexander screens from that organisation's Y-type body, two-piece glider doors and a large destination display. (David Toy Collection)

After purchasing 157 Atlanteans, Maidstone & District took delivery of 35 lowheight Daimler Fleetlines in 1963. A further 20 arrived in 1966 and this is last of them, DL 120 (FKL 120D). Note the driver topping up the radiator from a watering can. (STA)

Facing page: This drawing from *Bus and Coach* shows that the chassis of the Daimler Fleetline was not unlike the Atlantean. The Fleetline had conventional steel road springs, with a transverse positioned Gardner engine and a pneumocyclic gearbox with the same wheelbase as the Atlantean. This meant that body builders would not have to make major alterations to their body design for either chassis.
(Bus and Coach)

Daimler were able to capitalise in their advertising on the low step free entrance, and the flat floor on both decks which the drop-centre axle of the Fleetline made possible.
(David Toy collection both)

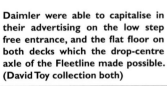
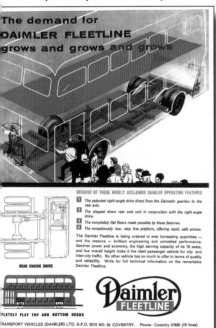
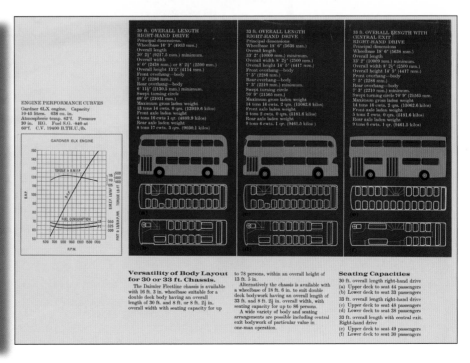

ENGINE PERFORMANCE CURVES
Gardner 6LX engine. Capacity 10·45 litres. 638 cu. in. Atmospheric temp. 62°f. Pressure 30 in. HG. Fuel S.G. ·840 at 60°f. C.V. 19400 B.TH.U./lb.

GARDNER 6LX ENGINE

30 ft. OVERALL LENGTH RIGHT-HAND DRIVE
Principal dimensions.
Wheelbase 16' 3" (4953 mm.)
Overall length
30' 2½" (9217.5 mm.) minimum.
Overall width
8' 0" (2438 mm.) or 8' 2½" (2500 mm.)
Overall height 13'5" (4114 mm.)
Front overhang—body
7' 5" (2286 mm.)
Rear overhang—body
6' 11½" (2130.5 mm.) minimum.
Swept turning circle
69' 0" (21031 mm.)
Maximum gross laden weight
13 tons 14 cwts. 0 qrs. (12919.6 kilos)
Front axle laden weight
4 tons 16 cwts 1 qr. (4889.9 kilos)
Rear axle laden weight
8 tons 17 cwts. 3 qrs. (9030.1 kilos)

33 ft. OVERALL LENGTH RIGHT-HAND DRIVE
Principal dimensions
Wheelbase 18' 6" (5638 mm.)
Overall length
33' 2" (10009 mm.) minimum.
Overall width 8' 2½" (2500 mm.)
Overall height 14' 5" (4417 mm.)
Front overhang—body
7' 5" (2286 mm.)
Rear overhang—body
7' 3" (2210 mm.) minimum.
Swept turning circle
70' 9" (21565 mm.)
Maximum gross laden weight
14 tons 16 cwts. 2 qrs. (15062.6 kilos)
Front axle laden weight
5 tons 2 cwts. 0 qrs. (5181.0 kilos)
Rear axle laden weight
9 tons 6 cwts. 1 qr. (9461.5 kilos)

33 ft. OVERALL LENGTH WITH CENTRAL EXIT RIGHT-HAND DRIVE
Principal dimensions
Wheelbase 18' 6" (5638 mm.)
Overall length
33' 2" (10009 mm.) minimum.
Overall width 8' 2½" (2500 mm.)
Overall height 14' 5" (4417 mm.)
Front overhang—body
7' 5" (2286 mm.)
Rear overhang—body
7' 3" (2210 mm.) minimum.
Swept turning circle 70' 9" (21565 mm.)
Maximum gross laden weight
14 tons 16 cwts. 2 qrs. (15062.6 kilos)
Front axle laden weight
5 tons 2 cwts. 0 qrs. (5181.0 kilos)
Rear axle laden weight
9 tons 6 cwts. 1 qr. (9461.5 kilos)

Versatility of Body Layout for 30 or 33 ft. Chassis.
The Daimler Fleetline chassis is available with 16 ft. 3 in. wheelbase suitable for a double deck body having an overall length of 30 ft. and 8 ft. or 8 ft. 2½ in. overall width with seating capacity for up to 78 persons, within an overall height of 13 ft. 5 in.
Alternatively the chassis is available with a wheelbase of 18 ft. 6 in. to suit double deck bodywork having an overall length of 33 ft. and 8 ft. 2½ in. overall width, with seating capacity for up to 86 persons.
A wide variety of body and seating arrangements are possible including central exit bodywork of particular value in one-man operation.

Seating Capacities
30 ft. overall length right-hand drive
(a) Upper deck to seat 44 passengers
(b) Lower deck to seat 33 passengers
33 ft. overall length right-hand drive
(c) Upper deck to seat 48 passengers
(d) Lower deck to seat 38 passengers
33 ft. overall length with central exit. Right-hand drive
(e) Upper deck to seat 49 passengers
(f) Lower deck to seat 30 passengers

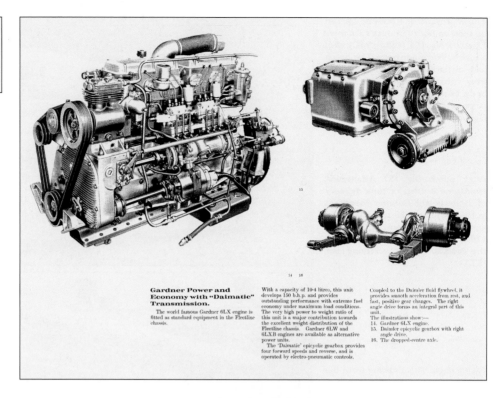

Gardner Power and Economy with "Daimatic" Transmission.

The world famous Gardner 6LX engine is fitted as standard equipment in the Fleetline chassis.

With a capacity of 10·4 litres, this unit develops 150 b.h.p. and provides outstanding performance with extreme fuel economy under maximum load conditions. The very high power to weight ratio of this unit is a major contribution towards the excellent weight distribution of the Fleetline chassis. Gardner 6LW and 6LXB engines are available as alternative power units.

The 'Daimatic' epicyclic gearbox provides four forward speeds and reverse, and is operated by electro-pneumatic controls.

Coupled to the Daimler fluid flywheel, it provides smooth acceleration from rest, and fast, positive gear changes. The right angle drive forms an integral part of this unit.

The illustrations show:—
14. Gardner 6LX engine.
15. Daimler epicyclic gearbox with right angle drive.
16. The dropped-centre axle.

Hants & Dorset, still a green fleet when this picture was taken in 1972, were amongst the former Tilling Group fleets operating Daimler Fleetlines; the six examples of which VRU 126J, 1903, is seen were bodied by Chas Roe of Leeds and had been ordered by Gosport & Fareham for the Provincial fleet. Roe were by this time building to Park Royal specifications and design since both bodybuilders were members of the ACV Group which also included AEC, Crossley and Maudslay. (John Senior)

BMMO D10

Another new double-deck chassis that had a high passenger capacity was shown in 1960 but not for general production. The Birmingham and Midland Motor Omnibus Company had been building its own vehicles for many years and had the rear entrance D9 in production. Two under-floor engined double-deckers were built; although it was never built to take on the Atlantean, it is its technology that is interesting. With an integral construction it had a front entrance with seating for 78. It used the in-house 10.5litre engine coupled to a four-speed pneumocyclic gearbox. In order to meet the ground clearance regulations the engine was turned with the cylinder heads facing inwards. This gave a low floor height of 2ft 3¼ins above the ground, there was a single step entrance. The D10 also had other interesting items for a double-decker, disc brakes at the front and Metalastic rubber suspension. Overall height was 14ft 4¼ins, headroom in both saloons were 5ft 11¼ins in the lower and 5ft 9¼ins in the upper. The complete vehicle weighed nearly half a ton less than an MCW-bodied Leyland Atlantean at 8ton 10½cwt.

Many years later Leyland produced the Lion double-decker with an underfloor engine, the D10 was advanced for its day. What would the industry have said if it had gone against the Atlantean?

The finished product, No. 4943 (943 KHA), with typical Midland Red body style, seating 78 passengers. Its sister bus was originally built with two staircases, with front and rear doors; this did not last long and the bus was converted to single-door and a single-staircase in 1962. (David Toy)

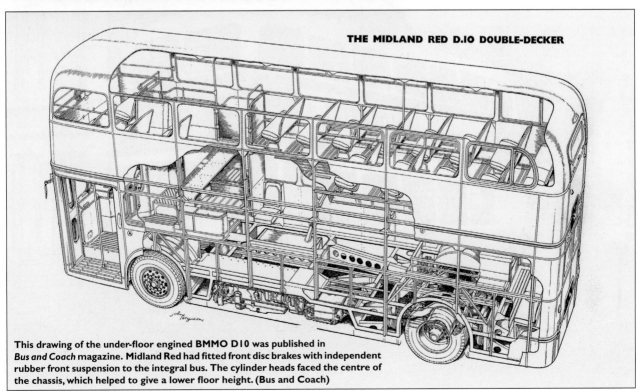

This drawing of the under-floor engined BMMO D10 was published in *Bus and Coach* magazine. Midland Red had fitted front disc brakes with independent rubber front suspension to the integral bus. The cylinder heads faced the centre of the chassis, which helped to give a lower floor height. (Bus and Coach)

THE MIDLAND RED D.10 DOUBLE-DECKER

Into the Sixties

The Atlantean had not tempted Southdown, the other large BET operator of the south. They were ordering Leyland PD3s with their own style of Northern Counties bodies. In the early 1960s, orders were slow from municipals but this was to change by 1963. Maidstone and District was ordering batches each year, as was Devon General. Devon General had routes that required vehicles with more power and had fitted turbochargers to a small number of their Atlanteans. I do not know if they had an agreement with Leyland but it did reduce engine life.

In 1960, both Devon General and Maidstone and District took further batches of Atlanteans with deliveries starting in April of that year. Some of Devon General's batch, DL895-917 (895-917 DTT), had offside illuminated advertisement panels fitted and these caused problems with flat batteries if they were left on without the engine running. The Roe bodies also gave problems with water leaking into the saloons when it rained; various modifications were carried out on the bodies including the strengthening of the floors. In later life, they suffered corrosion within the body structure, which led to their early withdrawal. The Maidstone and District vehicles were highbridge DH526-70 (526-50 HKJ/551-70 LKP) (no further lowbridge Atlanteans were purchased) to the same specification as the previous vehicles but with one less seat giving a total of 77. The Atlantean was becoming a familiar sight at most of their depots as the company was building one of the largest fleets in the country. The first municipal to order the Atlantean, Plymouth with 18 in 1960, ordered further batches bringing their total to 63 by 1963. The first of the second batch shown on page 19. During 1960 Portsmouth Corporation borrowed Maidstone and District's DH525 (525 DKT), one of the two coach-seated examples, for inspection. This led to them placing their first order for the Atlantean for delivery in 1963.

Brighton was unusual in operating half-cab double-deckers fo one-person-operation. This PD2/37 with forward entrance 196 built Weymann bodywork has been modified to allow the drive to collect the fares – notice the various signs.
(David Toy collection)

Portsmouth had built up an all-Leyland bus fleet with both PD and PD3 chassis. It also operated a trolleybus network and the fleet always looked smart in the maroon livery. Dating from 195 from the last batch of Leyland PD2/40s with a Metro-Cammel 56-seat body is No. 93 (LRV 985). Note the discreet gold linin still retained at this time. (Bob Rowe)

Silver Star's later vehicle deliveries had beadings on the side; these were the same as the Ribble Gay Hostess coaches. The fourth and final Atlantean, No. 42 (1013 MW), delivered in 1962 reverted to a 73-seat bus layout and has been preserved. (John Senior)

The third Silver Star Atlantean, No. 40 (XMW 706), had a Weymann 61-seat coach body and the upper deck of the coach-seated vehicle is seen here. It was purchased to extend the company's express services but the Traffic Commissioner refused the licence for the service and the vehicle reverted to private hire and stage services. (Jack Parsons/MCW)

Portsmouth took delivery of 35 Leyland PDR1/1 Mk2 Atlanteans with Metro-Cammell bodies between May and October 1963; these were purchased to replace the last of the town's trolleybuses. Painted in the traditional lined-out livery is No. 220 (220 BTP) with the standard style of Metro-Cammell body. (David Toy)

3 : The Mk2 Atlantean

There had been many problems with the early batches of Atlanteans as described earlier and Devon General went back to AEC for more Regent Vs for its next double-deck orders. Any move away from the Atlantean must have been a worry for the Leyland sales team. Leyland had not been idle and announced in 1963 the Mk2 version of the PDR1/1 Leyland Atlantean, which included modifications to overcome the majority of operator's problems. Maidstone and District started to upgrade their earlier vehicles to this specification. The main changes were:

- The engine and gearbox mounting brackets were now bolted; this meant that they could be removed as separate units.
- The standard Leyland O.600 engine had been up-rated to 130bhp at 1,800rpm.
- Rear-engine cowl was split into three with the corner panels bolted. It also had access hatches for the filling of water and the checking and filling of the engine oil.
- Self Changing Gears fluid flywheel with a lock-up clutch became standard in place of the centrifugal clutch.
- Repositioned gearbox electro-pneumatic control unit for easier accessibility and to keep it cooler.
- Front road springs uprated by 10%.
- Twin oil-bath air filters replacing paper elements.
- New long-life bonded rubber bushes for the torque stabilizer.
- Redesigned universal couplings on propeller shaft.
- Larger fan-drive shaft.

After taking rear-engined buses, Devon General reverted to forward-engined AEC Regents. (John Senior)

Leyland had an Atlantean in operation with Liverpool Corporation from 1961 to test the modifications. Maidstone and District's last batch of PDR1/1s were to the new specification with delivery starting early in 1963. The order was for 47, DH586-632 (586-632 UKM), and this brought the total to 157 in the fleet. Leyland began an advertising campaign for the Mk2 within the trade press. It must have received a shock that its largest customer in the south, Maidstone and District was turning to the new Daimler Fleetline with Northern Counties body for delivery starting in the last quarter of 1963.

Although this must have been a set-back there was the good news from Portsmouth Corporation who ordered 35 Atlanteans with Metro-Cammell bodies for the finish of their trolleybus replacement. Repeat orders came from Plymouth with 23 in 1963 and 8 in 1964. With the Daimler Fleetline in production and demonstrators being shown to the industry Leyland purchased a standard Leyland PDR1/1 Mk2 from Glasgow Corporation. It was fitted with the standard Glasgow Alexander body with 78 seats. It was shown to operators in the south and west including Devon General, Maidstone and District, Maidstone and Southampton Corporation.

In June 1963 Silver Star was sold to Wilts and Dorset Motor Services and three of the four Atlanteans were passed on to the Bristol Omnibus Company. This was the first time that a THC fleet had operated the Atlantean. The coach-seated vehicle No.409 (XMW 706) was sold to Super Coaches of Upminster. The Bristol vehicles were painted in Tilling green and cream and initially based at Western-super-Mare depot. These were the first rear-engined vehicles for the company and were a vast contrast to the standard Bristol Lodekka. In May 1963, Portsmouth took their first Atlanteans and they were in the traditional lined-out livery, which helped to offset the upright Metro-Cammell standard body. They had fluorescent interior lights in place of the standard

The last Leyland Atlanteans for Maidstone & District were 47 of the Mk2 version with Weymann bodies. In the centre of Maidstone is DH603 (603 UKM) from the last batch, overtaking DL75 (75 YKT), one of the newly delivered Northern Counties-bodied low-height Daimler Fleetlines. (M&D and East Kent Bus Club)

After being sold and with the star removed from the upper deck dome, No.7998 (VAM 944) looks very plain in its new Bristol Omnibus livery of Tilling green when compared with its original with Silver Star. These were the first Atlanteans to change ownership in the south and west and the first for a THC company to operate. (Jack Parsons)

Bournemouth had been loyal to Leyland with batches of Leyland PD2 and PD3 models. For a number of years it had bodies with dual entrance/exit which was unusual for this type of vehicle. New in 1959, Bournemouth No. 147 (YLJ 147) was one of ten Leyland PD3/1s with Weymann 62-seat dual-entrance bodies delivered that year. The improvement of body design can be seen on Leyland Atlantean No. 207 (HEL 207D) of the second batch with revised Metro-Cammell body. This batch had two piece glider doors and a large destination display. (David Toy collection both)

London Transport had large numbers of their specially designed AEC/Park Royal Routemaster which was a simple vehicle to maintain. They had full facilities to carry out major overhauls at their Aldenham works. Seen is an early Routemaster, RM 8 (VLT 8), a 64-seat bus delivered in 1959. (David Cole)

The Leyland Atlantean was a totally different concept and required revised thinking on maintenance for London Transport. Constant problems of overheating from coolant loss and flywheel glands led to the vehicle's early withdrawal. The whole batch of 50 was sold to China Motor Bus of Hong Kong in 1973. The last of the batch, XA50 (JLA 50D), stands new in a line up of London buses, waiting to cause heartaches when it enters service. (Colin Curtis collection)

London put eight Daimler Fleetlines into service in 1966 with the same body style as the Atlanteans, but none of the XA class survives. The Daimler Fleetline succeeded in making it into preservation and looking as good as new in this rear view is XF1 (CUV 51C), operating an enthusiasts' shuttle service from the (now closed) Cobham Bus Museum in April 1995. (John Senior)

The three section engine bonnet can be clearly seen on Portsmouth's No. 253 (ERV 253D) which entered service in 1966. The corner units were bolted and the centre section was hinged to give access to the engine and gearbox. The small hatch was for checking and the filling the engine oil. The earlier bonnet had to be raised to carry out checks and therefore the vehicles could not be parked too close together in the garage at night. (David Toy)

To show the industry the improvements with the Mk2 version of the PDR1/1 Atlantean, Leyland purchased from Glasgow Corporation one of their latest vehicles with an Alexander body in 1963 to use as a demonstrator. On trial under the trolleybus wires with Maidstone Corporation in May 1963 is SGD 669. Maidstone took their first Atlanteans two years later. The early Atlanteans delivered to Glasgow were badged as Albions to satisfy local pride! (M&D and East Kent Bus Club)

Not all Atlanteans would carry badges, and not all would be branded as Leylands. Some Scottish operators took vehicles masquerading as Albions, in a badge-engineering exercise supporting local industry, as seen below. (John Senior both)

bulbs. The Portsmouth trolleybus system came to an end on 27th July 1963 after 29 years of operation.

To overcome the low bridge problem and in order to compete with the Daimler Fleetline a new version of the Atlantean was introduced in 1964. The PDR1/2 had the Daimler gearbox with the dropped centre axle from the Albion Lowlander. This gave the bus a central gangway in both saloons with an overall height of 13ft 4ins.

Although Devon General had returned to AEC it did have Daimler Fleetline demonstrator 4559 VC with a Northern Counties body to try in June 1963. They did not go back to the Atlantean until 1966. Bournemouth was still operating trolleybuses and had purchased a new batch of Sunbeam MF2Bs with Weymann 65 seat dual-door bodies No.295-303 (295-303 LJ) in 1962. It was announced that the system would be run down over the next ten years. In late 1963, 20 Leyland Atlantean PDR1/1 Mk2 and 10 Daimler Fleetlines were ordered all with a new style of Weymann body. The style was not unlike the Alexander product with curved screens on both decks and seated 74. At the rear the bustle was shrouded by side covers. In 1966 the Fleetline order was increased to 20. The first Bournemouth Leyland Atlantean 179 (AEL 179B) was handed over on 9th November 1964. Further west, Plymouth was totally committed to the Atlantean and placed orders for a further 14 for delivery in 1965.

Leyland must have been very pleased when it received an order for 50 Leyland Atlanteans from London Transport for the Central area; they also ordered eight

Daimler Fleetlines for the Country Area. London had introduced large numbers of the AEC Park Royal Routemaster including the longer RML, seating 72. Being built to LT's own design the Routemaster had its maintenance system designed around the vehicle. The London Atlanteans were to have the larger Leyland O.680 engine, automatic transmission, power steering and power assisted handbrake. The body was by Park Royal with 72 seats (the same as an RML) and a standard product being based on the Stockton Corporation vehicles. The automatic transmission was by Self Changing Gears, this being a bolt-on system to the standard pneumocyclic gearbox. It was operated by a sensor on the propshaft, which sent signals to a control box. This had predetermined settings to gear change speeds and changed the gears automatically.

The vehicles XA1-50 (CUV 1-37C/JLA 38-50D) started to enter service on the 7th November 1965 on route 24 Hampstead Heath to Pimlico. London soon found that the Atlantean was not the best vehicle for their operation. Being used to the simple front-engined Routemaster with its high reliability and simple maintenance the Atlantean was a totally different concept and problems began to appear. With vehicles sitting in heavy traffic and slow running times the engine bay would become extremely hot and flywheels would overheat. This would lead to the gland failing with hot oil leaking onto the road and into the engine bay. The gearbox had to be removed to change the gland and the vehicle would be off the road for several days. Wear in the rod and ball-joint throttle system would cause problems with the automatic transmission and lead to the gear changing being very erratic. An internal report was published after two years of operation and it stated that there had been nine engine changes, 20 gearbox changes, 116 fluid-flywheel failures and 37 radiator failures during the period on the 50 buses.

Leyland had received an order from Maidstone Corporation for eight Leyland PDR1/1 Mk2 Atlanteans with Massey 74 seat highbridge bodywork. The Atlanteans were for the first stage of the Maidstone trolleybus replacement and would be Nos. 27-34 (EKP 227-34C). Fleet livery was brown and cream and this was to change with the Atlanteans. They were to have a new livery of Fiesta blue and cream and they entered service in November and December 1965. Devon General returned to the Atlantean in 1966 with an order for six, these had the larger O.680 engine for the hilly 104/5 routes at Paignton. They were Nos.526-31 (EOD 526-31D) with Willowbrook 75-seat bodywork. The previous Atlanteans that had turbochargers fitted for the routes had them removed, which helped to improve engine life.

Portsmouth and Bournemouth's trolleybus systems were separated by some 25 miles of coastline, but on one occasion in April 1967 they came together when preserved Portsmouth BUT number 313 ran on an enthusiasts tour in Bournemouth where it is seen alongside one of the native Weymann-bodied Sunbeam MF2B models. (Bob Rowe)

Maidstone had a small trolleybus network with Sunbeam W chassis with a mixture of Weymann, Roe and Northern Coachbuilders bodies. The exception was a pair of BUT 9611T chassis which came from Brighton Corporation in 1959 when they started to close their system. Shown here is Northern Coachbuilders No. 72 (HKR 11), built in 1947, the last trolleybus to operate in Maidstone and now preserved at The Trolleybus Museum, Sandtoft. (Bob Rowe)

Maidstone Corporation had been another loyal Leyland customer with batches of PD2/30 and PD2A/30 before turning to the Atlantean. The Corporation had used Massey as their main body supplier and No. 21 (21 UKK) is one of the former with a 61-seat rear-entrance body dating from 1961. Note the bus station, with East Kent and Maidstone & District vehicles. (Bob Rowe)

Their first Atlanteans were PDR1/1 Mk2 models delivered in 1965 and were in a new light blue and cream livery. The Massey body seated 74 but the style was very box-shaped and looked more upright than the MCW bodies on the Maidstone & District Atlanteans. Number 31 (EKP 231C) is showing off the new livery whilst operating alongside trolleybuses. (Bob Rowe)

Plymouth's later Leyland Atlanteans had a revised body style by Metro-Cammell–Weymann with a better frontal treatment. Delivered in 1967, PDR1/1 No. 206 (FJY 906E), the first of the batch, has a 75-seat body. (David Toy collection)

Bournemouth continued ordering PDR1/1 Atlanteans with Weymann Alexander look-alike bodywork. In the original livery, 1966 delivery No. 206 (HEL 206D) is seen at Christchurch. (Omnicolour)

In 1971 Portsmouth revised their livery, retaining the red but increasing the amount of white. Looking very smart is No. 243 (BBK 243B), a 1964 delivery Leyland PDR1/1 Atlantean with its Metro-Cammell 76-seat body. It is passing The Hard at Portsmouth. (David Toy)

Portsmouth took the roof from some of its 1966 Mk2 Atlanteans between 1977 and 1979, thus extending their lives, and number 9, formerly 250 (ERV 250D), is seen here at Clarence Pier; they replaced a similar number of PD2s which had been converted to open top and some of which survive in preservation. (John Senior)

An unusual customer for the Atlantean, BOAC purchased fifteen for their service between Victoria Air Terminal and Heathrow Airport. They had borrowed a Standerwick Gay Hostess Atlantean to evaluate the vehicle's suitability. One of these vehicles was shown at the 1966 Commercial Motor Show; the chassis was a PDR1/1 Mk2 with a O.680 engine in conjunction with a higher angle drive ratio which gave a high speed and very necessary good tractability.

The body was by Metro-Cammell with coach seating for 54, and this gave good leg room for the airline's passengers. A luggage compartment of 290cu ft was provided with a door in front of the engine compartment. The body style was the same as the Bournemouth vehicles but with a four-piece jack-knife door.

An unidentified Metro-Cammell bodied vehicle is seen leaving Victoria Air Terminal above, whilst on the left the classic Atlantean rear is shown, but with side shrouds and white windows to the large luggage pen at the rear of the lower saloon. It is travelling along the then two-lane M4 motorway before the major reconstruction of the late 1960s/early 1970s. The lower view shows LYR 307D, now preserved, at Dunsfold aerodrome in April 2011.
(John Senior all)

With the formation of British Airways in 1974 a new corporate livery of dark blue and white was introduced. Above LYF 317D, a 1966 Leyland Atlantean with the MCW body, was displayed at the Southsea Spectacular that year. (John Senior both)

Hall of Hounslow turned to the Atlantean PDR2/1 in 1969 with a Roe 68-seat body with extra luggage space for the airport contract for Trans World Airlines. Unlike the BOAC Atlanteans, Halls were fitted with bus seats, not quite the standard that airline passengers expected. Standing at Reading station, centre right, is VYH 47G in the TWA livery whilst below an unidentified member of the batch shows the rear aspect as it enters Heathrow airport.
(Mark Bailey, John Senior)

King Alfred of Winchester had 38 vehicles, including two rear-entrance 74-seat Park Royal-bodied AEC Bridgemaster B3RAs and two AEC Renowns. One of the latter (596 LCG) was photographed on an enthusiasts' running day in October 1995 whilst one of the Bridgemasters, former No. 107 (WCG 107), still in the original livery with crests, is seen parked in the yard, just after the takeover by Hants & Dorset in 1973.
(John Senior; David Toy)

King Alfred's last double-deckers were four Leyland Atlantean PDR1/2s with Roe bodies. These were repainted into poppy red after the purchase by Hants & Dorset in 1973.
(Omnicolour)

Devon General went back to the Atlantean in 1966 and purchased six, this time with Willowbrook 75-seat bodies. These were mainly for the 104 and 105 routes in Paignton and had the larger O.680 engine to help with the hilly terrain. With a full complement of opening windows in its Willowbrook body No. 530 (EOD 530D) looks very smart in its original livery. (Omnicolour)

Southampton had also been a Leyland customer and had taken PD2A/27s with very upright Park Royal bodies. In the centre of the city is No. 326 (326 AOW), new in 1962 with a 56-seat body. (David Toy)

Southampton City had also been an AEC customer, buying Regent Vs from 1962, and had taken 65 into the fleet, the last being delivered in 1967. Parked in the City Centre is No. 373 (FOW 378D) from the 1966 batch, fitted with an East Lancs 76-seat body. This batch had AEC AV690 engines; the earlier vehicles had the smaller AV590 unit. The more attractive shape of the ELCB body resulted in all subsequent orders being awarded to the Lancashire factory, as seen by the pair of Atlanteans awaiting their turn of duty in the background. (John Senior)

Southampton City took its first Atlanteans in 1968 with a batch of 20 with East Lancs bodies seating 76 on the PDR1/1 chassis. The livery was revised for these vehicles and No. 106 (OCR 150G) is waiting for passengers in Pound Tree Lane. A further 40 similar vehicles were delivered during the next three years, of which number 134 (TTR 168H) dating from 1970 is seen below and, by the looks of it, ready for a repaint. (David Toy; John Senior)

Foot of page: Devon General's last Atlanteans were delivered in 1968 and comprised 12 Mk2 models with Metro-Cammell bodywork of which No. 536 (NDV 536G) is seen here in glorious sunshine. (STA)

After purchasing Leyland Atlanteans and then Daimler Fleetlines, Maidstone & District turned to single-deckers and added 95 Leyland Panthers to the fleet between 1965 and 1968. They had Leyland O.600 engines at the rear with pneumocyclic gearboxes. The early batch had Willowbrook bodies and seen here is No. 3140 (LKT 140F) a PSUR1/1R from the last delivery with a Strachan 48-seat body dating from 1968. (David Toy)

Portsmouth Corporation went for the smaller Leyland model, the Panther Cub; this had the Leyland O.400 engine fitted at the rear. Twenty-six were purchased in 1967 seating 42 with 26 standees and two doors; there were two body suppliers, Marshall and MCW. Parked at Clarence Pier is number 162 (GTP 162E), the first Metro-Cammell-bodied example. (John Senior)

For their 1968/69 delivery Plymouth changed their body supplier to Park Royal on the longer PDR2/1 chassis. The body also had two doors with a seating capacity of 79. A further batch was delivered in 1971 and one of them, No. 10, (NDR 510J), is heading out of the city on route 44. (David Toy collection)

The FRM

London Transport, together with AEC and Park Royal, developed an integral double-decker based on the Routemaster concept. Leyland had merged with the ACV group, which included AEC and Park Royal, in 1962. Five chassis kits were produced but only one vehicle was ever built. Leyland had the Atlantean and there was no room for another vehicle with further development costs. The design had taken into account the layout and problems with the then current rear-engined buses that were in production. Although a bus for London, it was hoped that it would appeal to other operators. The industry was not in favour of integral vehicles and they would have to be convinced of this type of layout.

The FRM had an AEC 11.3litre AV691 engine rated at 150bhp at 1,800rpm, the gearbox was a four-speed fully automatic epicyclic, the same principle as the Routemaster. The gearbox was situated lower than other rear-engined chassis and the drive from the fluid flywheel went over the top of the gearbox. From here it went into a set of gears to the gearbox with a straight drive to the AEC rear axle. This arrangement was made with the objective to keep the flywheel and engine bay cooler and the main units could be removed individually. Front suspension was coil springs with wishbones and the rear was air. Braking was again the same as the Routemaster being full power hydraulic with a split system.

The body design and structure was the same principle as the Routemaster being aluminium, thus keeping the unladen weight down. Seating was for 72 and a road test carried out by *Bus and Coach Magazine* praised the performance of the FRM over other rear-engined vehicles. With its different suspension, it gave a very good ride compared to the Leyland Atlantean and Daimler Fleetline.

Times were changing and London Transport was about to turn to large capacity single-deckers for the future that would be one-person operated. Where London went others would follow, and orders for the Atlantean would reduce, until an upsurge back to the double-decker.

Leyland had purchased 25% of the shares of Bristol Commercial Vehicles in July 1966; Bristol was wholly owned by the Transport Holding Company and supplied only to their subsidiary companies. The Bristol product was going onto the open

market, but they did not have a rear-engined double-decker at that time. The Bristol RE was to become a challenge to the Leyland and AEC single-deckers and started to sell to BET companies as it had gained a good reliable reputation in service.

With Daimler offering a 33ft long Fleetline, Leyland introduced the same length Atlantean in late 1966, the model only being offered with the larger O.680 engine. From the 1st July 1966, one-person operation of double-deck vehicles was authorised for the industry and negotiations started in many areas with trade unions to implement the changes. Within the south and west, Brighton Corporation was the first to operate a one-person double-decker. Leyland PD2/37 No.23 (23 ACD) with a Metro-Cammell 64-seat front-entrance body was the first to be modified. Maidstone Corporation initially started to use their Atlanteans on Sunday operation for OPO.

The industry started to turn towards single-deck operation, London had ordered a fleet of one-person operated AEC Merlins and Swifts for both central and country garages. *The Reshaping of London's Bus Services* report had seen the single-decker as its future to accelerate the process of one-person operation. This was to be short lived and with a total of 1,503 new single-deckers in the fleet by 1972, London returned to the double-decker. Maidstone and District had ordered Leyland Panthers and later single-deck Daimler Fleetlines to speed up its one-person operation. Devon General was still purchasing double-deckers and ordered more Leyland Atlanteans for 1968. Of the municipals that operated Atlanteans only Portsmouth went down the single-deck road from 1967 with the Leyland Panther Cub and the AEC Swift.

A selection of views taken at Chiswick Works before FRM1 (KGY 4D) entered service; the curved windscreen gave it a better frontal style than the early Atlanteans. The rear was also neater than other rear-engined vehicles and the road test by the trade press of the time gave it a good write-up on its overall performance. The lower photo clearly shows the transmission layout, with the gearbox sitting lower than on other rear engined buses and the covered drive shaft above from the flywheel. The interior of the lower saloon is also shown before entering service.
(Colin Curtis/London Transport)

Bristol VR

Bristol Commercial Vehicles exhibited their new double-deck chassis at the 1966 Commercial Show, which was a 33ft side-engined double-decker. The engine was positioned longitudinally at the offside rear. It had a Gardner 6LX engine with a pneumocyclic gearbox where the drive went to a dropped centre axle. Two prototypes were built, both having Eastern Coach Works bodies and seating for 80. The position of the engine gave the vehicle a large rear overhang that could not be shortened. The vehicles went on demonstration to operators after the show and both ended up in the Bristol Omnibus fleet. There were export orders and Ribble used the chassis with Leyland engines for a fleet of double-deck coaches.

Bristol went back to the drawing board and in July 1967 announced the VRT chassis with a transverse engine with a close-coupled pneumocyclic gearbox. Although various engines were offered the Gardner 6LX range became the standard for the majority of operators. The gearbox had reduction gears that took the drive to a right-angled mitre box then from the prop shaft into a dropped centre axle. With this layout the body could be either low or full height. Unlike the other two rear-engine chassis on the market the VRT had a front-mounted radiator. Two chassis lengths and two frame heights were offered VRTSL being 30ft and VRTLL the 33ft version. Conventional steel road springs were used for the suspension with shock absorbers, braking was full air with spring brakes for parking. The engine compartment was built into the body and the whole rear-engine cover section hinged upwards for maintenance not unlike the early Atlantean.

In November 1967, the BET Group in which Aldershot and District, Devon General, Maidstone and District, Southdown and East Kent were subsidiaries sold out to the Transport Holding Company. The THC-owned companies within the south and west were Western National, Southern National, Hants and Dorset, Wilts and Dorset, Southern Vectis and Thames Valley. This would lead to changes in buying policy with Bristol now on the open market. From this merger the 1968 Transport Act would change the group into the National Bus Company as from the 1st January 1969. London was also changing with its control coming under the Greater London Council. The operations of the Country Division were to be passed to the new National Bus Company from the 1st January 1970.

In 1967, Leyland announced that the low-height Atlantean would have Leyland's own gearbox (in place of the Daimler unit) with a revised layout and to be known as the PDR1/3. Leyland also rationalised the gearboxes throughout the entire product range and the Atlantean became the PDR1A/1 for chassis built from July 1968. Daimler had become part of the Jaguar empire and in 1968, the holding company BMC joined Leyland to become the Leyland Motor Corporation. All the three rear-engined double-deckers were now under one holding company, as Leyland now owned 50% of Bristol Commercial Vehicles.

An official photograph of a VRL chassis with the Gardner 6LX engine positioned to the off-side at the rear. With the engine and transmission in this position the vehicle had a long rear overhang and a large amount of weight in one area. This layout, with its long rear overhang, was not liked by the industry and Bristol went back to the drawing board and came up with a transverse rear-engined chassis. (Bristol Commercial Vehicles)

Clearly showing the changes to the chassis is a plan view drawing of the 1967 Bristol VRTSL. There were now three rear-engined chassis on the market, and as Leyland by this time had a 50% shareholding in Bristol Commercial Vehicles the VRT would not be restricted to THC fleets. Instead it would soon be going into fleets all over the country – including Atlantean users in the south and west. (David Toy collection)

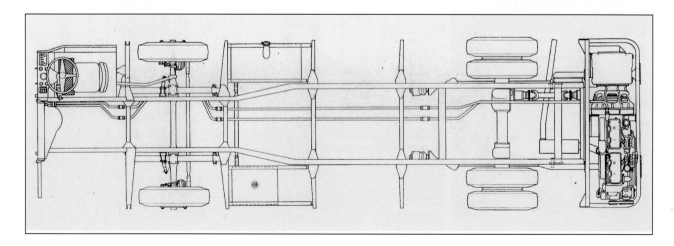

New customers were on the horizon from other municipals with one-person operation now going forward. Southampton ordered 20 PDR1/1s and Brighton ordered two batches of five Atlanteans. Bournemouth was still ordering each year and the Atlantean was moving along the south coast municipals.

The end came for the front-engined vehicles suitable for one-person-operation when the Government announced that a Bus Grant would be available to operators for the purchase of new buses from 1st September 1968. The grant was to be 25% of the purchase price for vehicles suitable for OPO. For double-deckers, this was based on rear-engined vehicles 9.5 or 10m in length, with the entrance under the control of the driver. This meant that only the Leyland Atlantean, Daimler Fleetline and the new Bristol VRT could meet the specification. Overnight this killed off the front-engined bus and Leyland dropped the PD2 and PD3 from its range. Operators were now going to take advantage of this including London, who were going back to the double-decker but not the Atlantean.

The happy times for the single-decker were not over as Leyland was planning, with the National Bus Company, a new integral single-decker to be produced at a new factory in Cumbria. Operators including London, who had turned to the rear-engined single-decker as the future, had hit major problems with body stress that led to cracking of the structure. Most first generation rear-engined single-deckers had a lighter chassis than their double-deck counterpart with the weight of the engine and gearbox suspended on the rear overhang. This led to chassis flexing and stress into the body. Many manufactures had to rework the rear end of their products in order to overcome this problem.

Leyland was also looking closely at the Atlantean chassis to update it and engineer out some of the continuing problems. The Fleetline had outsold it in 1968 and Leyland did not want the sales of the Atlantean to drop. The newly formed National Bus Company took the Bristol VRT as its standard double-decker but with the race on to save expenditure with one-person operation it would not be the only rear-engined double-decker to be purchased.

Southdown Motor Services, with its headquarters in Brighton, had stayed away from the rear-engined bus and had the largest fleet of Leyland PD3/4s all with full-front Northern Counties bodies. They were a loyal Leyland customer but their first rear-engined double-decker was to be the Bristol VRT with Eastern Coach Works body. With one-person operation becoming the norm Maidstone and District started to convert their fleet of Atlanteans and Fleetlines. This did not just mean fitting ticket machines, as a periscope had also to be installed in order for the driver to see the upper-deck. The emergency doors had to be fitted with a warning buzzer, which activated in the cab to draw attention to the driver that it had opened.

The Scottish Bus Group placed early orders for Bristol VRTs with Eastern Coach Works bodies and this official photograph shows AA286 (LFS 286F) prior to entering service with Eastern Scottish in 1968. The bodies on the Series I VRT were very plain, with flat windscreens, and clearly similar to the styling of the Lodekka built by the same bodybuilder. (Bristol Commercial Vehicles)

Bristol Commercial Vehicles lost no time in producing publicity pictures for the new model. (STA)

24A BRISTOL

EHU 365K

Relatively few of the municipal fleet operators ordered the Bristol VR. Reading had the distinction of being the only one in the south of England, where a total of 50 units, all with Northern Counties bodies, entered service between 1971 and 1974. (Bob Rowe)

TILEHURST

JUMP ON A JUMBO

XRD 22J

Since the Bristol VRT became the NBC's standard double-decker, it was only to be expected that most of the company fleets covered by this book would contain examples of the model. Southdown, Devon General and Western National representatives are seen here.
(STA all)

4 : Into the Seventies

Leyland was making continuing improvements to the Atlantean and was developing a revised version for introduction in the early seventies. In the first two years there were repeat orders for the PDR1A/1 Atlantean from Southampton, Bournemouth, Maidstone and the new order from Brighton Corporation. Plymouth now preferred the longer chassis and reordered the PDR2/1. The new National Bus Company was ordering the VRT for its south and west companies and working with Leyland on the new single-deck integral project. Leyland had anticipated that the industry was going down the single-deck road but this was changing with its largest customer (London) about to return to the double-decker. Municipals who had tried the single-deck experience were also returning which included Southampton, Brighton, Portsmouth and later NBC's London Country.

When London Country was separated from London Transport it became the largest of the NBC companies with 1,276 vehicles. It had a large problem with the inherited fleet. For such a prestigious company it had very few modern vehicles and only eleven double-deckers that could be one-person operated. The fleet included 484 RTs (AEC Regent III) and 209 Routemasters of various types. The single-deckers were no better with 413 RFs (AEC Regal IV). If NBC was to expedite one-person double-deck operation then large numbers of new vehicles were required. It was to turn to the Leyland Atlantean in a big way, taking its first in 1972. There were other changes within NBC from 1st January 1971 when Devon General became part of Western National. The Devon General fleet was painted into NBC Poppy Red as repaints became due.

After not purchasing Atlanteans for five years Portsmouth ordered twelve PDR2/1 chassis with Seddon 40-seat dual-door single-deck bodies Nos.188-99 (RTP 188/9J-TBK 190-9K) for delivery in 1971/2. These were the only single-deck Atlanteans that were purchased new in the south and west.

Brighton Corporation had built up a substantial fleet of Leyland PD2/37s with MCW bodies, the early ones being rear entrance. The later front entrance vehicles had been converted to one-person operation. Fourteen PD3/4s had been ordered but Brighton took only five, Nos. 31-5 (MCD 131-5F), cancelling the others and ordering ten PDR1A/1 Atlanteans. These had Willowbrook two-door 73-seat bodies Nos.81-5 (TUF 81-5J), delivered in 1971 and 86-90 (WUF 986-90K) in 1972.

The first ten Brighton AN68 Atlanteans were delivered in 1973. The fifth of the batch, No. 47 (CUF 147L), with a 73-seat Willowbrook dual-door body is at Old Steine in its original livery and fleetname style. (STA)

Brighton, as with other operators, turned to single-deckers and purchased seven Leyland PSURC1.1 Panther Cubs. Three had Strachan Paceline bodies and the other four were by Marshall. Seen is No. 42 (NUF 142G), the last of the Marshall vehicles, with a 42-seat dual-door body in the style used by the BET. The Panther Cub was found to be underpowered for Brighton's operations causing constant engine problems, and they were withdrawn after only seven years in service.
(David Toy collection)

Southdown had stayed with the front-engined double-decker and purchased a large fleet of Leyland PD3/4 and PD3/5 buses, all with Northern Counties bodies. This became a disadvantage when one-person-operated double-deckers were required. One of the 1967 batch, No. 347 (HCD 347E), with panoramic windows, is seen at Newhaven on its way to Seaford in the traditional Southdown livery.
(Southdown Enthusiasts Club)

In 1970, another rear-engined chassis type appeared in the Southdown fleet when 15 Daimler Fleetlines with Northern Counties bodywork were delivered. Two years later a further 15 Fleetlines were delivered, this time with Leyland engines and the by now familiar ECW bodies, and No. 391 (XUF 391K) is seen here in Brighton. (STA)

To speed up the conversion of services to driver-only operation, five Leyland Atlantean PDR1/3s with Alexander 73-seat bodies were transferred from Western Welsh to Western National in 1972. The vehicles were only a year old when transferred and in full NBC livery. Here Western National No. 1021 (VUH 378J) is seen loading passengers at Plymouth bus station. (David Toy)

London Country lacked driver-only double-deckers and eleven Daimler Fleetline CRL6 examples with Northern Counties two-door bodies seating 71 were diverted from Western Welsh in 1972. These became non-standard with the large intake of Atlanteans and were withdrawn in 1982. Looking smart in its first livery is AF10 (JPK 110K) on its way back to Reigate from Bromley.
(David Toy collection)

London Country's first Atlanteans were 90 Park Royal two-door models delivered in 1972. Number AN69 (JPL 169K) is seen in Stevenage. (STA)

Left: Eastbourne's dark blue and primrose livery was particularly attractive, and always well kept, and here it is shown to good advantage on preserved Regent V number 67 (KHC 367) seen at an AEC enthusiasts' rally in Nottingham. The later livery, seen below, did little to improve the appearance of these vehicles. (John Senior)

Below left: Eastbourne had purchased both the Leyland PD2 and the AEC Regent V and was a loyal customer of East Lancs Coachbuilders of Blackburn. The Corporation had stayed with a rear-entrance layout and parked in the depot at Churchdale Road is No. 63 (JJK 263), an AEC Regent V 2D3RV with 56-seat body dating from 1962. Its rather drunken-looking partner is No. 74 (BJK 674D), a Leyland PD2A/30 with a 60-seat body, one of 15 delivered in 1966. (David Toy)

Below right: As with others, Eastbourne tried single-deckers and purchased Leyland Panther PSU1A/1Rs and also Daimler Roadliner SRC6s, both with East Lancs bodies. Leyland Panther No. 7 (HHC 907J), new in 1971, has a 43-seat dual-door body. Parked next to it is Daimler Roadliner No. 90 (EJK 890F), new in 1968 and also with 45-seat dual-door body. The Panther was a more successful chassis than the Roadliner which used the Cummins V6 engine and was very unreliable. (David Toy)

astbourne's first Atlanteans were seven ...DR1A/1s with East Lancs 76-seat single-...oor bodywork. They had the same styling as ...uthampton but No. 16 (KHC 816K), looks ...ry bizarre in an all-over advert for Personal ...ervice Travel. (David Toy)

Portsmouth was the only operator to purchase the Atlantean as a new single-decker in the south and west. In its original livery, fully lined-out, is No. 191 (TBK 191K), a PDR2/1 with a Seddon 40-seat dual-door body. It stayed with Portsmouth until April 1982 when it was sold to the Portsmouth Harbour Authority. (STA)

Other single-deck driver-only vehicles were AEC Swifts with London Transport, which had the smaller AEC engine. Fitted with a Metro-Cammell 33-seat body with room for 27 standing is SMS619 (EGN 619J). (John Senior)

Side shrouds were fitted to many rear-engined vehicles, a classic example being the London Fleetlines as seen here on preserved example DMS 1818.
(John Senior)

London had gone back to the double-decker for one-person-operation and was to standardise on the Daimler Fleetline with Park Royal or Metro-Cammell-Weymann bodies. Ready to return to Hammersmith is DMS153 (JGF 153K), a 1971 CRG6 Fleetline with a Park Royal 68-seat two-door body with standing for 21 photographed in the snow at Hampton Court. (John Senior)

London had struggled on with its XA class of Leyland Atlanteans and in 1973 they were offered for sale. China Motor Bus of Hong Kong purchased the entire fleet and they kept the XA prefix. In Hong Kong the hilly terrain meant that they still had problems with overheating; CMB converted three of the Atlanteans (XA25, 44, 48) to Gardner 6LX engines. These were, as far as I know, the only Atlanteans to have this engine fitted. It was not an easy conversion and very costly. By the end of the seventies most of the batch had been removed from service, but a small number lasted into 1980.

Leyland had shown its new single-deck integral at the 1970 Commercial Motor Show and it was now a joint venture with the National Bus Company. The company became Bus Manufactures (Holding) Ltd and also acquired the 100% share capital of Bristol Commercial Vehicles, Eastern Coach Works and the Leyland National Company. NBC needed to replace large numbers of its fleet and 498 Nationals were ordered for the Group with delivery in 1972 and in the first quarter of 1973. Leyland had high hopes for the Leyland National as it projected that the industry was turning to single-deck operation.

Policies were changing with Bus Grant for double-deck one-person operation and London, finding that its experiments with high capacity single-deckers had not worked, was going back to the double-decker. This was also happening in a number of companies in the south and west. With the Bristol VRT being the standard NBC double-deck chassis that could accommodate both full and low height and the Fleetline outselling the Atlantean with the London order, the future for the Atlantean did not look good.

Engineers had been wary of the early problems with the Atlantean and Leyland started to make changes to the PDR1A/1. A new version was to be introduced, the AN68, which would only use the larger 11.3litre O.680 engine. Changes had been made to the engine by using the CAV rotary fuel pump in place of the inline unit. It would be offered with two power ratings, 153 and 165 BHP. The AN68 was not to be a completely new chassis but a revised Atlantean that had engineered out many of the earlier problems. Leyland implemented the changes in a gradual way and several PDR1A/1s (known as Specials) had some of the new AN68 specification and were delivered to NBC companies as part of their order.

With the country enduring severe industrial unrest in 1973/74 and with many industries on a three-day week this affected the production lines at Leyland and at the bodybuilders. By 1974 Leyland was deeply in debt.

After NBC was formed it was not long before the new logo and fleetnames began to appear on the side of the vehicles. Standing in Maidstone for the return journey back to Gillingham and the long climb up Bluebell Hill is No. 5520 (520 DKT), a 1959 Leyland Atlantean with a Metro-Cammell body. (M&D and East Kent Bus Club)

Working the same group of routes as the previous vehicle and from the same batch is No. 5499 (499 DKT). Painted in the new NBC livery, but wearing the original Maidstone & District logo, was probably not what group headquarters really wanted. (M&D and East Kent Bus Club)

Fully refurbished is former Maidstone & District No. 5567 (567 LKP), a 1960 Leyland Atlantean PDR1/1 with Metro-Cammell body and re-seated to 76. Now No. 3999 in the Hants & Dorset fleet it moved to Western National in 1977, being withdrawn in 1981 after giving 21 years of service for three operators. (Jack Parsons)

In April 1975 several of the low-height Leyland Atlantean PDR1/1s with Weymann bodies were transferred to Western National from Maidstone & District. Former DL51 (51 DKT) started life in the Hastings area in 1959 as a trolleybus replacement, and became No. 1046 with Western National. (M&D and East Kent Bus Club)

Devon General colours were changing too and No. 929 (929 GTA), Sir Richard Grenville, a 1961 Leyland PDR1/1 with Metro-Cammell convertible open-top body is now in the revised NBC livery for the class which was applied during 1972. (David Toy)

NBC poppy red is now the colour and gone is the traditional Devon General livery. Number 529 (EOD 529D), a 1966-built Leyland Atlantean PDR1/1 Mk2 with Willowbrook 75-seat body, has a reasonable loading. (David Toy collection)

In May 1973 the Maidstone & District garage at Ashford was transferred to East Kent. This included a number of Leyland Atlantean PDR1/1s with Metro-Cammell bodies. Standing inside the garage in its new poppy red livery is ex-M & D DH571 (571 RKJ) alongside an East Kent Regent V. (David Toy)

Western National was another NBC company that had early PDR1/1 Atlanteans transferred to them from Maidstone & District. Dating from 1959, ex-DH521 (521 DKT) of M&D with a Metro-Cammell 76-seat body became fleet No. 996 with its new owner. (Omnicolour)

Leyland AN68

Large steps were taking place in vehicle design where bodybuilders were changing to operators requirements. One of the leaders was Greater Manchester Buses and with Harry Taylor's influence their Leyland Atlanteans and Fleetlines all had a standard body, built either by Northern Counties or Park Royal. This change included an improved environment for the driver and electrical systems. GM Buses No. 7602 was demonstrated to Southampton City Transport for them to try the G2 automatic transmission. Brighton Borough was the first in the south and west to have its own design of cab and electrical systems although it was not as neat as GMB's because Brighton was a low production run due to its small fleet. However, many smaller operators benefited from the improvements introduced by the larger operators.

The chassis had many modifications over the earlier version and was only to be offered as a full height chassis and two body lengths of 30ft 10ins and 33ft 3ins. This left the low height options to the Daimler Fleetline and the Bristol VRT. The main changes were:

*   Modified main chassis frame with a front cross member.
*   The front overhang lengthened in order to give a wider door aperture.
*   Rear overhang increased in order that bodybuilders can fit back-to-back seating over the rear wheel arch.
*   Cable operated throttle in place of rods.
*   Spring brakes for parking in place of conventional handbrake.
*   Stainless steel air piping with a neater layout.
*   Power steering as standard on the longer chassis and an option on the shorter.
*   Increased capacity in the cooling system with larger header tank.
*   Radiator alarm system fitted for low coolant with warnings in the cab and at the rear.
*   Remote engine start within the engine bay with a safety system to isolate the front starting button when the engine hood was opened.
*   A new three-piece engine cowl with side-hinged swing-out doors. They were located by spring-loaded location pins.
*   Fully charged fluid coupling with common oil for the four-speed pneumocyclic gearbox, flywheel and angle drive. This was to help reduce operating temperatures of the units.

This Leyland publicity photograph shows one of the 1,250 SELNEC/Greater Manchester PTE standards, this one with Park Royal built bodywork has a modified windscreen adopted after extensive trials to reduce the amount of road spray – and dirt – which collected on the body sides. The new shape changed the air flow around the front of the vehicle and moved the spray rearwards. Northern Counties were the main supplier and helped develop these vehicles, one of their examples seen following. (DSH collection)

As this photograph shows, Greater Manchester PTE improved the driver's area on their Atlantean and Fleetlines with a new dash panel and improved electrical systems designed by Northern Counties. During the 1970s the smaller municipal operators gained from these changes and specified them on their buses. (David Toy)

Maidstone & District also took Leyland Atlanteans PDR1A/1R specials with Metro-Cammell bodywork; 20 were diverted from Midland Red in 1972. Parked in Gillingham depot is No. 5710 (FKM 710L) with a better looking body style than the early Metro-Cammell batches. (David Toy)

The standard PRV/Roe design was instantly recognisable with the slightly angled upper-deck window lines. This Park Royal-built example was delivered to Southdown in 1974, becoming their No. 709 (PUF 139M) and is seen working when new on the 55 service between Upper Portslade and East Saltdean, a Brighton Area Transport Service. (Mervyn Stedman)

Two NBC operators in the south and west had the Leyland Atlantean PDR1A/1 Specials, London Country and Maidstone and District. London Country needed to replace the RTs and RMs to reduce costs and accelerate driver only operation. Maidstone and District took 20 from a diverted order from Midland Red. These chassis did not have the fully charged coupling but had the other main changes of the AN68.

In 1973/4 industrial unrest affected the lead time on chassis and bodies whilst the revision of the Bus Grant pushed up demand. Operators had to order well in advance and as the first Leyland AN68s went into service around the country they found that the changes made by Leyland had improved reliability. The AN68 also began to gain export sales with 500 for Baghdad again putting pressure on production.

Leyland started to look to the future, and with the integral single-deck National in production its eyes turned to the double-deck market with the thoughts of an integral double-decker that would replace their existing range. Seminars were held with the operators in late 1972 on the concept of an integral double-decker code-named B15. This was to be 14ft 5ins high with independent air suspension at the front. The brakes were to be full power hydraulic and also a hydraulically operated gearbox. The engine was to be the fixed head 500 series as used in horizontal form in the new Leyland National. With the reorganisation of the Leyland Group there were growing delays in chassis delivery. With the thought that Leyland was going to set its plans on an integral double-decker body manufacturers could see a limited future for their own bodies.

MCW had produced an integral single-decker as a joint venture with Scania, but it had sold in limited numbers. To help increase business and give operators another choice MCW began to develop a double-deck version of the Scania/MCW combination.

The revised Atlantean was gaining orders from the municipals in the south and west. London Country was also placing orders for the AN68 with Park Royal bodies after taking 120 of the PDR1A/1 version. East Lancashire Coachbuilders of Blackburn had repeat orders from Southampton, Eastbourne and Brighton as a new customer. The two latter operators were to take the revised East Lancs style of body. Southdown also had the AN68 on order; it was one of the few companies that were to operate the Atlantean, Fleetline and the VRT from new. The National

For a number of years the Southsea Spectacular was a major transport event supported by many southern operators. Southampton chose East Lancs to body all its Atlanteans and number 200 (HTR 569P) is seen here leaving the common in 1976. (John Senior)

After purchasing batches of single-deckers, Portsmouth returned to double-deckers in 1972, with a change of body allegiance to Alexander. These additions to the fleet were on Leyland Atlantean AN68/1R chassis and were fitted with 75-seats and two doors. Parked on display at Southsea is No. 274 (XTP 274L) from the 1973 delivery looking very good in a special advertising livery. (John Senior)

Above: London Country's varied fleet included some RTs which looked far less impressive in service than this preserved example, RT 604, HLX 421, seen here at Dunsfold aerodrome, might suggest. (John Senior)

Top right: With the exception of its eight Daimler Fleetlines, all the double-deck vehicles were crew operated at the start of NBC London Country and the Routemaster had the majority of double-deck operation. Dating from 1965 AEC Park Royal Routemaster RCL2255 (CUV 255C), a former Green Line vehicle, is waiting to return to Crawley. (David Toy collection)

When London Country was formed on 1st January 1970 it had a very elderly fleet, including many of the RF class dating from the early fifties. Repainted into its new NBC livery is RF65 (LYF 416), an AEC Regal IV with Metro-Cammell 39-seat body, which has a good loading on service 489. (David Toy collection)

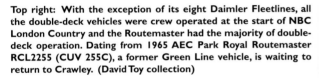

Other single-deck driver-only vehicles were AEC Merlin 4P2Rs, which had the larger AEC 691 engine. Fitted with a Metro-Cammell 33-seat body with room for 27 standing is MBS438 (VLW 438G). (David Toy collection)

London Country also had Metro-Cammell two-door bodies on the Leyland Atlantean PDR1A/1 Specials. Seen here is AN118 (MPJ 218L) a Crawley based vehicle delivered in 1974. (David Toy)

London Country turned to the Leyland Atlantean and took 120 PDR1A/1R Specials with a mixture of Park Royal and Metro-Cammell bodies. This is an official photograph of AN30 (JPL 130K) with the new style NBC 72-seat two-door Park Royal body. For its first batches the London style of destination screen was specified.
(Park Royal Vehicles/ STA)

The Park Royal body for London Country had two doors with a centre staircase, and both decks are shown in the two official photographs.
(Park Royal Vehicles/STA)

Bus Company had ordered the AN68 with a revised Park Royal body; the same style was also produced at Roe.

The government had increased the grant for one-person only operation to 50%. Operators were now ordering to take advantage of this and increase their OPO for both double and single-deck vehicles. Southdown had taken large numbers of their own full-front body style by Northern Counties on the Leyland PD3/4 and PD3/5 and now needed to increase their OPO requirement. Bristol VRTs were entering the fleet with 41 Park Royal Leyland Atlantean AN68/1Rs to the standard NBC design.

Southdown's full-fronted Leyland Titan PD3s were impressive and reliable vehicles, being nick named Queen Marys. Waiting in Pool Valley Brighton is No. 832 (VUF 832) delivered in 1959, about to work service 12 to Eastbourne. It will work hard climbing the long hill from Seven Sisters. (MD Woods)

After purchasing Atlanteans for several years, Plymouth turned to the Leyland National. Seen when quite new at the Hoe is No. 26 (SCO 426L), a rather grubby Leyland National 1151/2R0202 with dual-door layout and seating for 46. Plymouth purchased Leyland Nationals from 1972 to 1974 before returning to the Atlantean. (STA)

Brighton Corporation had ten Leyland AN68/1Rs with Willowbrook bodies delivered in 1974, having standardised on a two-door layout. This batch had a short life, No. 48 (CUF 148L) being sold in 1985 after only eleven years in service. (Willowbrook)

As shown here, the interior was rather sombre and uninviting, with plain leather-cloth, whilst bench seats were used on the lower deck between the doors. (Willowbrook)

Before changing direction to a single-deck fleet, Maidstone Corporation took four Leyland Atlantean AN68/1R examples with Northern Counties bodywork in 1972. The third of the batch, No. 53 (EKR 153L), is on its way to Park Wood Estate, a former trolleybus destination. (M&D and East Kent Bus Club)

Maidstone & District had turned to the standard NBC double-decker, the Bristol VRT, after taking Atlanteans and Fleetlines. Seen in Tunbridge Wells is No. 5825 (RKO 815M), a VRT/SL2/6LX with a 77-seat Eastern Coach Works body new in 1973. (M&D and East Kent Bus Club)

Two different front end styles on East Lancashire bodies on AN68/IRs. Southampton stayed with the curved windscreens for all its deliveries and No.186 (PCR 309M) from the 1974 batch is seen right. Eastbourne changed to the flat screen with a three-piece front lower panel. Seen at Southsea Bus Rally is No.21 (GHC 521N) in the year it was delivered, 1975. The two different styles can be clearly seen with a Southampton vehicle parked next to it. (David Toy, both)

The Leyland Atlantean came back into the NBC fleets with a standard body built either by Park Royal or Roe. Seen here is Southdown No. 738 (SUF 138N), an AN68/IR with a Park Royal 73-seat body delivered in September 1974 and repainted in 1977 for the Queen's Jubilee. The AN68s were used on the longer distance services as shown here on the 700 from Brighton to Portsmouth. Later they were seen in most of the Southdown area. (David Toy)

When London Country disposed of the three XA class Atlanteans to Hong Kong in conjunction with London Transport's 47, they needed replacements. Three Leyland AN68/IRs were ordered; these were the first AN68s for the company and became the standard double-decker over the following years. In a move away from London practice they had standard NBC destination screens. Looking very smart in its NBC livery is the first, AN121 (VPB 121M), delivered in May 1974, with a two-door Park Royal body with 71-seats. (David Toy collection)

The interior of the lower deck of a Brighton East Lancs-bodied Atlantean of the Nos. 53-62 batch. Later vehicles had soft trim in place of the leathercloth seats and improvements to the interior panelling. (David Toy)

Brighton turned to East Lancs Coachbuilders having taken 20 Willowbrook bodies on their first Atlanteans. Leyland Atlantean No. 60 (JFG 360N), an AN68/1R, has a 73-seat two-door body and had the exit door positioned close behind the front axle. (David Toy collection)

Portsmouth continued to take Alexander bodies with the distinctive peaks and two doors on its Leyland Atlanteans. From the 1975 batch No. 308 (HOR 308N) is seen passing two of Southdown's Park Royal-bodied AN68s. For the following year's delivery Portsmouth turned to the Leyland National. (Southdown Enthusiasts Club)

Plymouth had modified its livery and like a number of operators had found the Leyland AN68 a good reliable bus. After purchasing Leyland Nationals for the last three orders it went back to double-deckers with Park Royal or Roe NBC style of bodywork. Parked in the depot is No. 133 (STK 133T) with a Roe 74-seat single-door body from the 1979 batch. See also the facing page for a later Plymouth livery. (David Toy collection)

Southdown took six further Leyland Atlantean AN68/1Rs in 1975 with the standard NBC PRV-designed Roe-built body. Looking better designed than the Bristol/ECW combination No. 743 (LCD 43P) is parked at Hilsea. (David Toy collection)

A line of East Kent's Leyland Atlantean AN68/1Rs at Dover depot. Fifteen were delivered in 1976 with ECW full-height 74-seat bodies. The style was the standard body for the Bristol VRT and was not as appealing as the Park Royal/Roe bodies for NBC. (David Toy)

The Leyland Atlantean became the backbone of the London Country double-deck fleet with deliveries up to 1981 of 293 chassis. All the AN68s had either Park Royal or Roe bodies and could been seen all over the network. Crawley had a major service revision in July 1978 with routes introduced starting with a 'C'. Crawley based AN134 (UPK 134S), an AN68A/1R with Park Royal 73-seat body and new in April 1978 is on the local C5 service. (David Toy)

Plymouth continued to take East Lancashire bodies with curved screens, but now with a single door. Seen in the centre of Plymouth is No. 169 (TTT 169X) a Leyland Atlantean AN68C/1R delivered in 1981, now rebranded as Plymouth City Bus. (Harry Postlethwaite)

5 : Leyland Faces Renewed Competition

The Ailsa

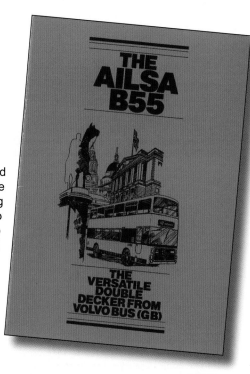

In 1974 a new front-engined chassis was announced that had been developed in conjunction with the Scottish Bus Group. It was first shown in its complete form in 1974 at the Scottish Bus Show in Glasgow as the Ailsa B55. Being different from other chassis it had the engine at the front and used the Volvo 6.7litre TD70 unit with a pneumocyclic gearbox. With operators being used to the Leyland 11.3litre or the Gardner 10.45litre engines, the concept of a small turbocharged engine developing up to 201bhp was completely new. By using such an arrangement it overcame one of the major drawbacks of Guy's Wulfrunian – namely its heavy Gardner engine. The Ailsa was shown to operators in the south at a Bus Conference in Brighton in October 1974 when Greater Glasgow's first vehicle AV1 was demonstrated to conference delegates. There were only two operators who took the Ailsa from new in the south and west and only in very small numbers. Maidstone & District had five for the NBC tests at Hastings and later London Buses had Ailsas in their test programme.

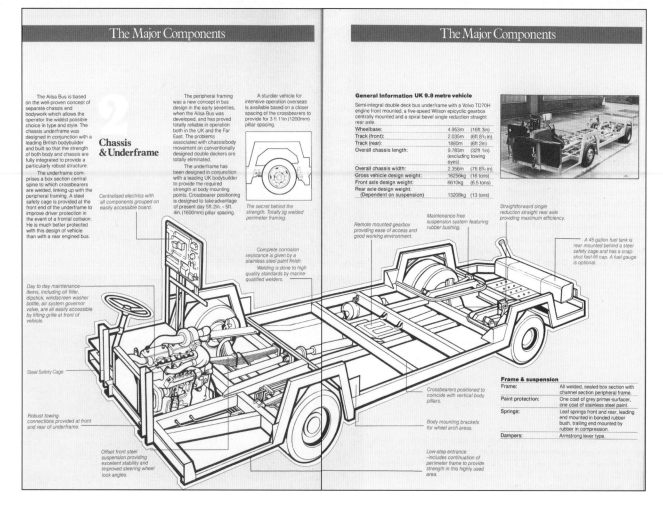

The Major Components

The Ailsa Bus is based on the well-proven concept of separate chassis and bodywork which allows the operator the widest possible choice in type and style. The chassis underframe was designed in conjunction with a leading British bodybuilder and built so that the strength of both body and chassis are fully integrated to provide a particularly robust structure.

The underframe comprises a box section central spine to which crossbearers are welded, linking up with the peripheral framing. A steel safety cage is provided at the front end of the underframe to improve driver protection in the event of a frontal collision. He is much better protected with this design of vehicle than with a rear engined bus.

Chassis & Underframe

Centralised electrics with all components grouped on easily accessible board.

The peripheral framing was a new concept in bus design in the early seventies, when the Ailsa Bus was developed, and has proved totally reliable in operation both in the UK and the Far East. The problems associated with chassis/body movement on conventionally designed double deckers are totally eliminated.

The underframe has been designed in conjunction with a leading UK bodybuilder to provide the required strength at body mounting points. Crossbearer positioning is designed to take advantage of present day 5ft.2in. - 5ft. 4in. (1600mm) pillar spacing.

A sturdier vehicle for intensive operation overseas is available based on a closer spacing of the crossbearers to provide for 3 ft 11in (1200mm) pillar spacing.

The secret behind the strength. Totally jig welded perimeter framing.

Complete corrosion resistance is given by a stainless steel paint finish.
Welding is done to high quality standards by marine-qualified welders.

Day to day maintenance items, including oil filler, dipstick, windscreen washer bottle, air system governor valve, are all easily accessible by lifting grille at front of vehicle.

Steel Safety Cage

Robust towing connections provided at front and rear of underframe.

Offset front steel suspension providing excellent stability and improved steering wheel lock angles.

General Information UK 9.8 metre vehicle

Semi-integral double deck bus underframe with a Volvo TD70H engine front mounted, a five-speed Wilson epicyclic gearbox centrally mounted and a spiral bevel single reduction straight rear axle.

Wheelbase:	4.953m (16ft 3in)
Track (front):	2.035m (6ft 8½ in)
Track (rear):	1880m (6ft 2in)
Overall chassis length:	9.783m (32ft 1in) (excluding towing eyes)
Overall chassis width:	2.356m (7ft 8¾ in)
Gross vehicle design weight:	16256kg (16 tons)
Front axle design weight:	6610kg (6.5 tons)
Rear axle design weight: (Dependent on suspension)	13208kg (13 tons)

Straightforward single reduction straight rear axle providing maximum efficiency.

Remote mounted gearbox providing ease of access and good working environment.

Maintenance-free suspension system featuring rubber bushing.

A 45-gallon fuel tank is rear mounted behind a steel safety cage and has a snap-shut fast-fill cap. A fuel gauge is optional.

Crossbearers positioned to coincide with vertical body pillars.

Body mounting brackets for wheel arch areas.

Low-step entrance –includes continuation of perimeter frame to provide strength in this highly used area.

Frame & suspension

Frame:	All welded, sealed box section with channel section peripheral frame.
Paint protection:	One coat of grey primer-surfacer, one coat of stainless steel paint.
Springs:	Leaf springs front and rear, leading end mounted in bonded rubber bush, trailing end mounted by rubber in compression.
Dampers:	Armstrong lever type.

Parked in Brighton Borough's Lewes Road depot is an unregistered Ailsa B55 with an Alexander body. Greater Glasgow AV1 was demonstrated to delegates at the 1974 Bus Conference which was held in the town. (David Toy)

In 1975 Maidstone & District took five Ailsa B55 10s with Alexander 79-seat bodies for comparative trials at Hastings. They were evaluated against the Scania Metropolitan and the standard NBC Bristol ECW combination. The last of the batch is shown above, No. 5385 (LKP 385P); they were later moved to the Medway towns. (John Senior)

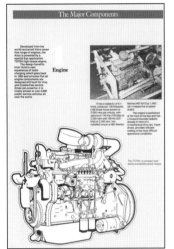

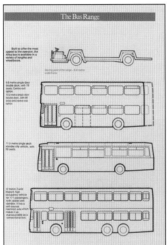

London Transport took three Volvo Ailsas for experimental purposes. The third of these, No. V3 was unique in having twin doors, one at the rear as shown, and twin staircases in the Alexander bodywork.
(David Cole both)

MCW's Metropolitan

In late 1973 MCW announced a double-deck version of their single-deck Scania-based integral. With the future looking uncertain for bodybuilders after Leyland had announced the development of the B15, MCW was to offer an alternative.

The Metropolitan was based on the Scania BR111DH, which used the D11 11litre engine rated at 200bhp. The transmission was Scania's own two speed unit and this was the first rear-engined double-deck to enter service with full air suspension. An MCW integral steel-framed body was fitted with its own distinctive asymmetrical windscreen layout. Working with Leyland in the past MCW had experience of integral vehicle construction with single-deckers. With 200bhp available, the vehicle could accelerate very fast and drivers had to get used to its lively performance. The steering was also very light when compared to other vehicles on the market. The Metropolitan was the first of a new generation to challenge the Atlantean and its other Leyland stablemates. The vehicle was purchased by Leicester and most of the PTEs. In the south and west Reading Transport was an earlier purchaser, having built up a fleet of Bristol VRs and in its first year in 1975 MCW captured 10% of the market. Maidstone and District took five vehicles in 1975 as part of an NBC trial against the other new vehicle, the Ailsa B55, and its own Bristol VRT. This was initially carried out in the Hastings area then moved onto the Medway towns. In 1976, London Transport started to take 164 Metropolitans, which was a total contrast to the DMS Fleetline. The Scania gearbox became its main problem with a short life and later corrosion in the body.

In 1975, Leyland rationalised the gearboxes over their range and the Leyland AN68 gained a five-speed close ratio gearbox. The Atlantean became the AN68A/1R or AN68A/2R for the longer chassis. The other major development was Leyland's improved bolt on electrical control system for automatic transmission known as G2. This had a kick-down and manual hold for third and fourth gears. It also controlled

London Transport took delivery of 164 MCW Metropolitans, but they had a very short life and they were all taken out of service by June 1983. Captured in London's Park Lane is MD101 (OUC 101R) one of the vehicles delivered in 1977 to London Transport with a 72-seat dual-door body. (John Senior)

the throttle during the gear change, which gave a smoother change. The fuel and electrical company CAV had also developed an automatic control system and was updating it, it was not unlike the Leyland G2; this was to become the CAV 511 gear control system.

Although the Leyland AN68 Atlantean had entered service with very few delivery defects, service problems began to appear. The throttle was operated by a cable (PDR versions had rods) but with no lubrication points it had a tendency to stick. If automatic gear control was fitted it gave a very jerky gear change. Leyland developed various types of cable for operators to try. It was not totally resolved until an air throttle was fitted on the AN68B/1R version. Some operators fitted a Williams' air throttle kit on the early AN68s. The automatic brake adjusters began to fail allowing the brakes to back off. This led to an internal redesign of the adjuster, which overcame the problem. The radiator mounting had also been troublesome with the early vehicles and this passed over to the AN68, so Leyland produced a revised mounting with a stay bar.

Leyland was also moving the Fleetline construction from Coventry to Leyland, which totally disrupted production. With the large order from London Buses and Hong Kong this did not help the supply of Fleetlines to its customers. In the south, a new NBC customer for the Atlantean was East Kent with an order for 15 AN68/1R with ECW 73-seat bodies, 1-15 (JJP 1-15P). They had purchased the AEC Regent V and Daimler Fleetline in the past as their double-deck chassis.

MCW built a demonstrator which was registered NVP 533M and is seen here whilst with Greater Glasgow PTE. (STA)

Reading No.1 (GRX 1N), a MCW Metropolitan delivered in 1975 with a 73-seat dual-door body, cost the Transport Department £23,000. Reading went on to purchase 32 more new examples together with several second hand examples from London Buses and Tyne & Wear PTE. (David Toy)

An early purchaser of the Metropolitan was Leicester City Transport. (David Cole)

Maidstone & District had five 75-seater single-door Metropolitans delivered in 1975 and they started their life in the Hastings area. The fourth vehicle from the batch is in its first month's service in the photograph of No. 5254 (KKO 254P), below; the position of the off-side radiator can be clearly seen. This allocation was part of the NBC tests on new generation vehicles; they were all moved later to the Medway towns.
(M&D and East Kent Bus Club)

Dennis Dominator

With the problems of long delivery times from Leyland and their dominance in the market, Dennis, after being out of bus production for several years, looked again at building a new chassis. Many operators were concerned at Leyland's plan to produce an integral vehicle as its replacement for the double-decker. Dennis purchased a second-hand ex-Leeds City Transport Daimler CVG6LX and fitted it with a German Voith 3-speed fully automatic gearbox which had a built-in retarder. This was shown to the industry and found that there were very positive comments for this type of transmission.

The Dennis Dominator was born aimed directly as a replacement for the Leyland Fleetline customers. It would have a Gardner 6LXB engine with a Voith D581 gearbox which would drive a dropped centre axle, making it suitable for low-height operation. Suspension was to be kept simple with steel leaf springs; the braking system was new to the industry being the Girling full air Twin Stop system. The Twin Stop had been used by Ford in their Transcontinental truck range.

The chassis was designed to be either double or single-deck; it had a very sturdy structure. The Gardner 6LXB engine (Dennis were offering the Rolls Royce Eagle as an option) was fitted transversely at the rear with the Voith D581 gearbox. It had a set of gears on the offside that took the drive to a shaft that went into a bevel box and then into the dropped centre axle. Dennis had been cautious with the suspension and stayed with leaf springs. Due to the time needed to get the chassis into production air suspension was not offered, which was at the time unique to other second generation double-deck chassis. The later Mk3 chassis offered this option and it became standard to all the chassis. For the driver power steering was standard and the chassis was offered in three lengths. The prototype Dominator had an East Lancs Coachbuilders body in the same style as fitted to the Atlantean and it was later registered as SHE 722S. The adoption of a South Yorkshire registration reflected the substantial input made by SYPTE into the development of this bus, which, with a Rolls Royce engine, became their standard vehicle.

Day in, day out,

A new concept in bus chassis design

This new Dennis Dominator chassis has been designed for economical operation, to lower fuel and maintenance costs, and to give a smooth, safe ride. All this, plus versatility of specification and the general strength and reliability normally associated with Dennis products make this a bus chassis unique in its class.

With reduced brake wear

The Dennis custom built chassis incorporates the Voith automatic transmission with built-in hydraulic retarder, which is not only safer but results in significant savings in brake wear – the hydraulic retarder is wear-free and its use gives considerable savings on maintenance costs.

The front of the first brochure for the Dennis Dominator. The bus shown is Brighton's new No. 71 (OYJ 71R), a Leyland Atlantean AN68A/1R with an East Lancs body. The prototype Dominator was not finished in time for the brochure so Dennis borrowed the Atlantean and modified the front for the photo. (Dennis)

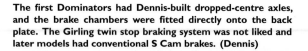

The first Dominators had Dennis-built dropped-centre axles, and the brake chambers were fitted directly onto the back plate. The Girling twin stop braking system was not liked and later models had conventional S Cam brakes. (Dennis)

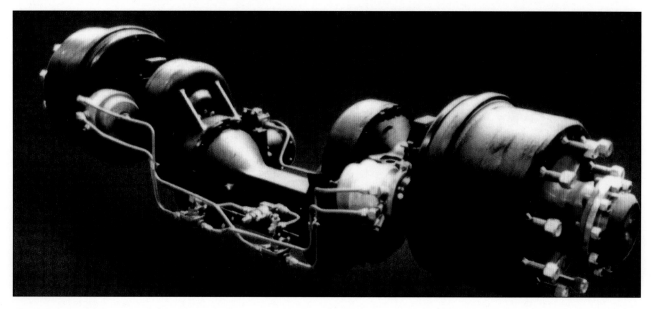

Above: Some rather amateurish retouching is evident in the brochure Dennis produced for the new Dominator. (Dennis)

Upper right: A detailed photograph showing the drop-down box attached to the Voith gearbox that took the drive to the rear axle via a bevel box. (David Toy)

Centre, lower: Two views of the prototype Dennis Dominator taken in Brighton, before being registered as SHE 722S. The author, who was then Chief Engineer at Brighton, had the opportunity to drive the new vehicle and found the retarder very impressive. At Brighton it was shown to the senior managers of bus operators who were there for a conference. The body, by East Lancashire Coachbuilders, was of the same style as fitted to Atlanteans except for the rear-end treatment which was much neater. (David Toy)

Top left: One of the first customers for the Dennis Dominator was Leicester City Transport, having them bodied by East Lancs. Seen at the 1978 Hillingdon Bus rally is Leicester's No. 237 (UFP 237S). (David Toy)

Top right: Maidstone & District was again used as a testbed by the NBC for new double-deckers. Six Dennis Dominator DD129s with an unusual choice of Willowbrook bodies, seating 74, entered service in 1980. The third member of the batch, No. 5303 (FKM 303V), is seen on a rail replacement service. (David Toy collection)

Left: Eastbourne had been a loyal Leyland customer but turned to Dennis for its next generation vehicles. Brand new is No. 39 (MPN 139W), a Dennis Dominator DD120 with an East Lancs 74-seat body, photographed before entering service in 1981. (David Toy)

Next door at Brighton they also turned to the Dennis Dominator DDA134 with East Lancs 74-seat body. Brighton's were Mk3 versions with air suspension and a straight rear axle. Seen at Southsea before entering service is No. 17 (OAP 17W) in 1981. (John Senior)

6 : The Next Generation

In the late 1970s, the Atlantean, with its improved reliability, was selling well to most of the Passenger Transport Authorities and municipals around the country. Leyland had gained large export orders for the AN68 Atlantean including a small number to the USA. In the south and west, Brighton had 15 in 1978; Southampton had standardised on the AN68 Atlantean and continued to place orders; Portsmouth and Plymouth's last Atlantean orders were for East Lancs bodies. Eastbourne only took a small number and had turned to the longer AN68/2R. The National Bus Company had stopped purchasing the Atlantean for the southern companies with the exception of London Country. The Bristol VRT was the standard double-decker with ECW body for NBC.

MCW had come away from their agreement with Scania after producing 659 complete vehicles for the home market and decided to produce their own integral vehicle, the Metrobus, a direct challenge to the Leyland Titan. The prototype was built in 1977 and had a Gardner 6LXB engine with a Voith D581 fully automatic gearbox with a built-in retarder. The suspension was full air with an option of either full air or full power hydraulic brakes. The body followed its MCW predecessor with a dropped near side windscreen. It could be either a single or two door configurations. London Transport ordered a trial batch of 50 to compare against the Leyland Titan and this was increased to 200 when the Titan order was also moved up to 250.

Further trials were to be carried out at Maidstone and District in 1980 for NBC with the new MCW Metrobus and Dennis Dominator, the B15 with its new name of Titan was to be included but, due to delivery delays, it was cancelled. Leyland had a major problem with Titan production and London's increase in its order added to this. The industry wanted a chassis that would offer low-height and was still cautious about the integral vehicle.

All the Leyland rear-engined chassis were coming to the end of their useful life but Leyland continued to update the AN68. In 1979, the AN68B was introduced, this had the Friedmann and Maier inline fuel pump with Amback injectors in place of the CAV DPA unit. To overcome the continuing throttle problems an air throttle was introduced. The G2 automatic gear control system was replaced with the new LAV45 system, which had the latest electronics. The AN68B had the automatic gear control as standard but Leyland changed things very quickly to the AN68C model that had semi-automatic control. The "B" version had a very short production run, but for a time all three models were in production at the same time. The Leyland rear-engined range was to be reduced to two with the Fleetline production being terminated in 1981. Some of the last chassis went to Bournemouth. In the interim until the new B45 chassis was fully available low-height demands were to be left to the Bristol VRT.

Eastbourne started to look at new generation chassis and ordered the Dennis Dominator for delivery in 1981. Brighton followed with an order for two of the new Mk3 chassis with air suspension. Leyland showed its new double-deck B45 chassis at the 1980 show at Birmingham with the name of Olympian; as long as there was still a demand for the Atlantean, Leyland stated that it would stay in production.

With the change of Government in May 1979 came new philosophies to have an open market. There was to be a easing of the road service licensing and the new Transport Bill would deregulate coach services. Coach deregulation day was on the 6th October 1980 which allowed operators to compete with the NBC network.

All the NBC companies in the south and west had their own central workshops, which catered for the major overhaul of their fleets. These workshops overhauled the engines, gearboxes and vehicle ancillary equipment; they also had body repair and paint shops. The municipals had the same facilities but on a smaller scale. Buses and coaches had to have a Certificate of Fitness, which was issued by the Department of Transport. A new vehicle would be issued with a seven year certificate and at its expiry it would be recertified by a Certifying Officer. Depending on the vehicle's condition a new certificate would be issued for five or six years. As the vehicle became older this would reduce and in some cases only a one

In 1977 MCW produced a rationalised design of its Metropolitan known as the Metrobus. London's M1 (THX 101S) was the first MCW Metrobus DR101/3 with a 69-seat two-door body, seen here parked at the 1978 London Bus rally. (David Toy collection)

Seen at the same rally the following year is Reading's first Metrobus DR102/8, which also had a 69-seat body. At both Rallies Brighton No. 10, a Leyland AN68A/1R with East Lancs body, was judged the best modern vehicle in each year. (David Toy)

Maidstone & District had five MCW Metrobuses for the NBC test programme and they had various combinations of engines and braking systems. Fitted with a Rolls Royce Eagle engine and full power hydraulic braking is No. 5269 (FKM 269V) operating on a local Medway Towns service and which entered service in 1980. (M&D and East Kent Bus Club)

THE COMPANY WE KEEP

MCW's high reputation in the road passenger vehicle manufacturing industry is sustained by its record of

year in year out achievement of a high level of acceptance of its products throughout the world over a long period. This success is earned by the Company's active response to the changing needs of progressive and discerning customers in the passenger vehicle operating industry who continuously demand the best available products to serve their travelling public in terms of accessibility, comfort and safety

plus contributing to the preservation of the general environment. MCW also responds effectively to the operators' needs of dedicated manufacturer technical and service support throughout the usable life of vehicles. Typical of such users of MCW products are the few examples whose emblems appear below.

A colourful piece of advertising literature showing the wide range of operators taking the Metrobus, both in the UK, including London and all the PTEs. There were also some prominent overseas customers including those in Hong Kong. (STA)

Seen at Duxford, now in preservation, is M1000, giving an indication of the size of intake of this model in the London fleet – in fact, there were nearly 1,500. The board in the windscreen records the fact that this has a Gardner engine, much less thirsty than the Scania engine in the Metropolitan. (David Cole)

With London Country struggling to meet service due to the unavailability of its fleet, it hired in from other operators. Maidstone Borough was changing its fleet to a single-deck one and had surplus Leyland Atlanteans with Massey bodies. These were hired to London Country and Maidstone No. 35 (JKE 335E) is operating the 403 looking out of place in its blue livery. (M&D and East Kent Bus Club)

In 1975 a surprise order from Maidstone Borough was for Bedford YRQ and YRT models with Willowbrook 45-seat bodies. Number 57 (HKJ 257N), a YRQ seen left, was one of the first of the new order as Maidstone turned away from the Atlantean to lightweight chassis. (David Toy)

Maidstone had turned to high floor single-deckers on medium weight Bedford chassis in 1975 but it also purchased six Leyland Leopard PSU3B/4Rs with Duple dual-purpose bodies from Nottingham City Transport that were only one year old. Eight more were purchased from the same source the next year. These had been part of the famous 'Lilac Leopard' Park-and-Ride fleet. The last of the first batch, No. 222 (HNU 122N), is seen later in life after it had been renumbered from No. 22. (David Toy)

London Transport took Leyland Nationals after their problems with AEC Swifts and Merlins. Here LS24 (KJD 524P) is seen after being purchased for preservation and splendidly turned out at Dunsfold in 2011. (John Senior)

Portsmouth was another operator who returned to the single-decker for its next order. Fourteen Leyland National 10351/2R were delivered in 1976 with 38-seat two-door bodies. On its way to The Hard, where Nelson's flagship the Victory can be seen, is fleet No.111 (KCR 111P), looking very smart in the Portsmouth livery. (David Toy collection)

As with other NBC companies, Devon General turned to single-deckers as replacements for double-deckers on some routes. One of the first for the company was No. 234 (GFJ 662N), a Leyland National 11351/2R with two doors, seating 44 and delivered in 1974. (David Toy)

Southdown also took Leyland Nationals. Here No. 59 (UFG 59S) is at North Street, Brighton, working a local service. This was one of the shorter versions, delivered in 1977, with two doors, seating 44 passengers and carrying 25 standees. (David Toy collection)

year certificate might be given. Vehicles were subject to an annual inspection at the company premises by the Ministry of Transport Vehicle Inspectors but not all vehicles were checked. The central works was used to prepare vehicles for recertification which usually included a repaint. With this system decisions were often made on when to dispose of a vehicle due to its body/chassis condition or reliability. Recertification could be a high expenditure, as a very high standard of preparation was expected.

The EEC issued a directive in 1977 that all PSVs were to follow the HGV industry with annual testing which had to be introduced by 1982. The test centre would be the same as the HGVs or on operator's premises if they had the appropriate equipment. This was to be the end of regular certification; a vehicle would hold this from new. The new test would not be as stringent as certification on body work. A Certifying Office could ask for panels to be removed on the body to check the under structure and corrosion, but in the new system this would not happen. Where operators might dispose of vehicles after 12 to 15 years the new system could allow a vehicle to go on indefinitely. In some companies, the Atlantean was to stay in service with its original owner for more than 20 years. Over the next two decades, second-hand Atlanteans would appear in companies who would not have operated vehicles of that age on front line service. With Atlantean production being in its twilight in the early 1980s the Leyland Atlantean was going to be around for many more years and re-appear in London. Leyland had got the AN68 right and the orders were still coming in.

Seen in Southampton city centre is No. 354 (OJI 1874) a rebodied 1975 AN68/1R with an East Lancashire Sprint 35-seat single-decker body. Five of the early Leyland Atlantean AN68s of Southampton had their double-deck bodies removed and replaced in 1971. For their length they had a small seating capacity and were a heavy vehicle as a single-decker. (David Toy collection)

Plymouth began to amass a large fleet of Leyland Atlantean AN68A/1R vehicles which had NBC-style bodies. Delivered in May 1979, No. 128 (STK 128T) has a Roe 71-seat two-door body and is seen in the centre of the town. (Harry Postlethwaite)

This brand new Leyland Atlantean AN68A/1R for Southampton City Transport, No. 242 (UPO 242T), is seen parked outside the old East Lancashire Coachbuilders factory in Whalley Road, Blackburn in March 1979. (East Lancashire Coachbuilders)

Portsmouth also continued to purchase AN68A/1R Atlanteans with Alexander two-door bodywork. On its way to Southsea is No. 325 (UOR 325T), which entered service in December 1978. (Southdown Enthusiasts Club)

As well as taking the Leyland Atlantean, London Country was to build up the largest fleet of Leyland Nationals in order to remove Routemasters and the RF class of single-deckers. An example from the 1978 delivery was SNB258 (NPK 258R), a short 41-seat bus version. (David Toy collection)

Maidstone & District had an increased requirement for double-deckers and took twelve Daimler Fleetline CRG6LX with Alexander 77-seat bodies in 1972. These were built in 1969 and were transferred from Northern General who took the same number of Daimler Fleetline single-deckers from M&D in exchange. Waiting to return to the Medway towns from Maidstone on service 29, which was an indirect route though the Medway valley villages, is No. 5008 (GCN 810G). (David Toy collection)

The last 400 Leyland Fleetlines for London Transport had the quiet pack and were designated as the B20 and the majority were fitted with a lightly turbocharged Leyland O.680 engine. At the rear they had large air scoops with fans for the engine. Above is DMS 2365 (OJD 365R), which was fitted with a Park Royal body. (David Toy collection)

Left: One of the standard DMS class, DMS 1818 (GHM 868N), is seen here smartly turned out in preservation, looking better than most of the class did during much of their time in service when they became so unpopular that mass disposals once again became the order of the day, providing the rest of the industry with a ready supply of useful and reliable vehicles at knock-down prices. This is a Leyland-engined example. (John Senior)

Brighton's last new Leyland Atlanteans were 15 AN68A/1Rs with East Lancs 74-seat single-door bodies delivered in 1978. Standing at Old Steine is No.10 (TYJ 10S) on its way to Brighton Station from Saltdean. Photographed in 1980, No.10 has a revised livery with an Oxford Blue skirt. (David Toy)

Brighton Corporation was the first operator in the south and west to have its own specification for its cab layout in place of the standard Leyland binnacle; this was on the later East Lancs bodies. Shown below is the cab of No. 67 (OYJ 67R), one of the two-door batch. (David Toy)

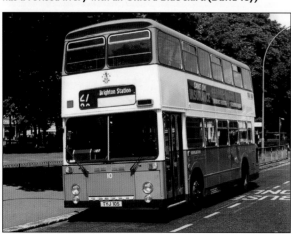

A very happy author (who was Chief Engineer at the time), stands in front of Brighton's No. 10 (TYJ 10S) at the Show Bus Rally at Uxbridge in 1978 after it had won best in class for new vehicles. (David Toy collection)

Right: No more new Atlanteans for Maidstone & District were delivered and it subsequently received the standard Bristol VRT SL3 with ECW bodywork. In the centre of Tunbridge Wells is No. 5844 (BKE 844T), a November 1978 vehicle. (David Toy collection)

Below: Eastbourne continued its allegiance to East Lancs by taking four of the longer AN68A/2R chassis with seating for 82 in 1978. The first of the batch, No. 28 (VDY 528T), is seen later in its career. (David Toy)

Below right: Bournemouth turned away from Leyland Atlanteans but stayed with the Fleetline. It received a batch of convertible open-top Leyland Fleetline FE30ALRs with Alexander bodies which were delivered in 1978. Bournemouth's No. 138 (VJT 138S) is in its summer guise with the roof removed. (David Toy)

The Leyland Atlantean could still be seen in London on sightseeing tours as seen above. When the TWA contract finished LLH 6K, a 1972 PDR2/1 with a Roe 69-seat body, moved to Limebourne for the Cityrama tours. (David Toy)

Brighton had a requirement for five Atlanteans when four Leyland PD3/4s were converted to open top. Five Leyland Atlantean PDR1A/1s with Northern Counties 76-seat two-door bodies were purchased from Nottingham City in 1979. Former Nottingham No. 504, new in February 1969, became Brighton's No. 76 (PTO 504G). It is seen here on road test before entering service. However, they were unpopular with drivers and only lasted until 1981. (David Toy)

The Leyland B15

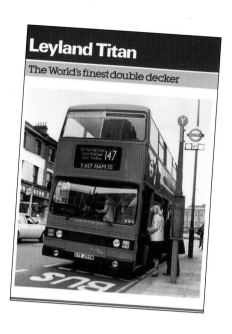

The B15 was to replace the current range of Leyland double-deckers and was a leap in technology with experience gained from the Leyland National. The engine was the vertical 500 series with a hydraulically operated gearbox that could have fully- or semi-automatic control. The power steering was by rack and pinion, and suspension was full-air, a first on a Leyland double-deck vehicle. Braking was a full power hydraulic system which London buses used on the Routemaster. London was not going to rush into orders and wanted a long test programme; it was still taking delivery of the DMS class of Daimler Fleetline.

The industry had never rushed into the integral vehicle, and only London and Midland Red had experience of this type of construction. Limited orders were placed by PTEs and NBC, but due to industrial problems at Park Royal delivery times became so protracted that most were cancelled and only a small number went to operators outside of the capital. London stayed firm, however, and next ordered 50 with Gardner 6LXB engines which was soon increased by a further order for 200.

The body design continued the boxy shape of the Fleetline Londoner, and soon became widespread with the B15 and its successor Olympians threading their way through the streets of the capital. It was, however, to became a major factor in the closure of two of Leyland's factories as traditionally-skilled bodybuilders refused to adopt the engineered concept which they described – not without justification – as Meccano construction. It was designed to be capable of assembly using partially, or mainly, semi-skilled labour and that was not acceptable to the trade unions or their members. Attempting to impose this in a London factory was not one of Leyland's more astute moves.

The B15, or as it was later named Titan, was planned to be built at Park Royal Vehicles in north London, but due to Leyland's escalating labour problems it decided to close the factory. Attempts to move production to Eastern Coach Works were rebuffed equally robustly. After the first 250 for London, production was therefore

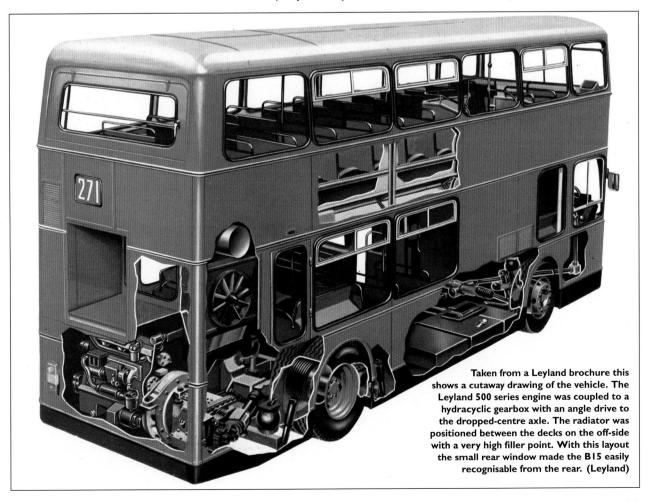

Taken from a Leyland brochure this shows a cutaway drawing of the vehicle. The Leyland 500 series engine was coupled to a hydracyclic gearbox with an angle drive to the dropped-centre axle. The radiator was positioned between the decks on the off-side with a very high filler point. With this layout the small rear window made the B15 easily recognisable from the rear. (Leyland)

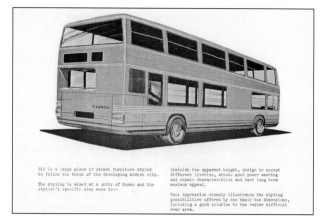

B15 is a large piece of street furniture styled
to follow the theme of the developing modern city.

The styling is aimed at a unity of theme and the
stylist's specific aims were to:-

Diminish the apparent height, design to accept
different liveries, attain good power washing
and repair characteristics and have long term
maximum appeal.

This impression clearly illustrates the styling
possibilities offered by the basic box dimensions,
including a good solution to the rather difficult
rear area.

B15 is a large piece of street furniture styled
to follow the theme of the developing modern city.

The styling is aimed at a unity of theme and the
stylist's specific aims were to:-

Diminish the apparent height, design to accept
different liveries, attain good power washing
and repair characteristics and have long term
maximum appeal.

This impression clearly illustrates the styling
possibilities offered by the basic box dimensions,
including a good solution to the rather difficult
rear area.

Air-ride suspension

It's air suspension all round on the bus, with
a low frequency ride that guarantees maximum
passenger comfort, and wide based springing for
maximum stability in handling. The system
incorporates automatic levelling so that constant
step height is maintained regardless of vehicle
load.

Suspension is independent at the front with
substantial vertical wheel travel ensuring a well
cushioned ride. It also provides considerably

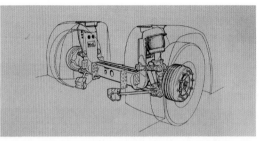

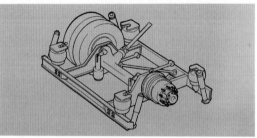

higher roll stiffness on cornering and a low
front gangway height. The stiff integral body
structure makes for accurate wheel alignment
with precise handling control, due to the
rigidity of the suspension mounting points. At
the rear end a wide based H-frame carries four
air-bellows units, one at each corner, giving
maximum stability and a broad spread of input
loading across the structure. Outrigger dampers

All suspension location linkages are
bushed to prevent ride harshness and
outstanding reliability with the minim
maintenance. At the front end, torsio
support most of the tare weight while
springing suspends the additional pass
The air springs provide near constant
frequency ride motion and are piped
system of levelling valves which autor
level the vehicle fore-aft and crosswis

An important aspect of air suspens
contribution to considerably reduced
ance. Air bellows are generally more di
than leaf springs and are cheaper and
to replace when required.

Specially posed for an early Leyland brochure, Leyland B15-04
prototype (NHG 732P) is supposedly working the busy 24 route
in London from Victoria to Hampstead Heath though the lack of
any passengers confirms it is not actually in service. It entered
service trials on 26th May 1976 from Chalk Farm garage and had
a two-door layout seating 71. (Leyland)

LEYLAND TITAN

a new horizon
in public transport

Facing page top: Drawings of Leyland's B15 project double-decker for the future were shown to the industry in 1972. (Leyland)

Facing page centre: The B15 was a totally different concept from previous Leyland double-deck buses. There was a prototype Leyland Atlantean in 1956 that had many of the same items but was rejected by the industry on cost. (Leyland)

Facing page, lower right: When Greater Manchester PTE finally received its Titans it took only a small batch of just 15, having originally placed a substantial order for 120 which as explained elsewhere Leyland could not fulfil; GNF 6V subsequently passed to Swindon & District and is seen here at Bristol Docks. (John Senior)

moved to a new facility within the Workington Leyland National plant. This brought in unacceptable delays and allowed a reappraisal by operators of the complexities of the Titan, which had clearly been designed with London Transport very much in mind, and also of Leyland's many problems. In the event, Greater Manchester received 15 from the 120 originally ordered; West Midlands took 5; Greater Glasgow and West Yorkshire's were both cancelled with Reading's 12 being the only others outside London Transport.

Orders for the Atlantean were still very buoyant throughout the industry, but it would not be able to meet forthcoming legislation, and so Leyland transferred its efforts to a chassised vehicle which would encompass some of the virtues of the B15 Titan and recover some of its investment whilst being more acceptable to operators through less sophisticated engineering and the ability to be bodied by a wider variety of bodybuilders.

Above: London began to take Leyland Titans into its fleet in large numbers in 1979, but delivered the previous year was T2 (THX 402S) which had seating for 68 and is seen here on a Rail Replacement Service. (David Toy collection)

London Transport's T6 has been preserved and restored to its original condition. Here it gleams in the sun at the Showbus Rally at Duxford. (David Cole)

The Replacement Arrives

With new European legislation pending on braking, engine noise and emissions Leyland needed to have a new rear-engined chassis to compete with other manufacturers and also have a chassis that would have a separate body. The Titan had only sold to London in large numbers and Reading Transport was the only other customer who took any above a trial number. Leyland developed a new chassis in under twelve months at the Bristol plant. The chassis was to replace all the first generation chassis including the Atlantean. Both the Fleetline and the Bristol VRT would cease production in 1981, the Atlantean would continue for UK production until 1984.

Code named B45 it was launched at the 1980 Motor Show and named Olympian. The chassis differed from all the first generation models by having a perimeter frame that was in three sections and would allow different lengths. Gone was the independent front suspension of the Titan and a conventional axle was in its place, with full air suspension using locating springs to hold it in place: the rear section with Leyland's dropped axle was the same as the Titan. The engine and gearbox was supported from a rail at waist level in the engine bay. Two engines were offered: the new Leyland TL11 rated at 170bhp and the Gardner 6LXB rated at 177bhp. There were no options on the transmission, only the Leyland five-speed Hydracyclic gearbox. The gearbox was hydraulically operated and had an integral retarder. With two lengths of wheelbase on offer, 16ft 3ins and 18ft 6ins, and having the ability to have a low-height body, the Olympian could meet most operators' requirements.

Leyland had also revamped the Leyland National and introduced the Mk2 version. This had a Leyland O.680 engine in place of the unreliable 500 series. The radiator was moved to the front and the exterior styling was changed but the orders for the National were declining. The last version of the Leyland Atlantean was the AN68D introduced in 1982 when Leyland rationalised the O.680 engine in line with the TL11 engine, this included changes to the cylinder heads, which could not be interchanged with the early O.680 engine. The last new Atlanteans for the south and west were for Plymouth and Southampton who purchased the AN68C version. London Country took only one of this type, and was the only NBC company to take this version new into their fleet within the area.

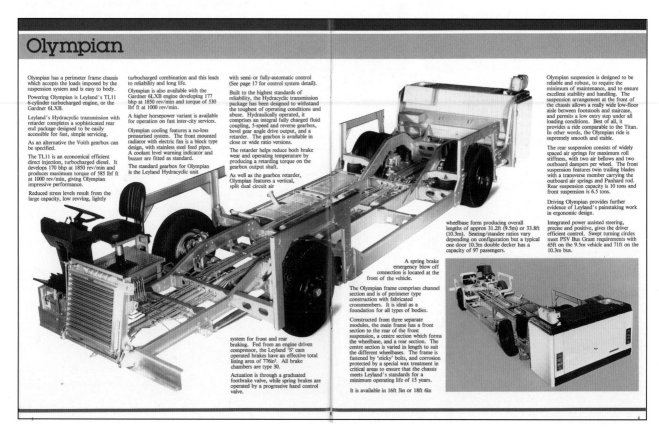

Above: The fourth prototype Leyland Olympian which was shown at the 1980 Bus and Coach Show was in Midland Scottish livery. It was transferred to Northern Scottish in 1981 as their NLO1 (OMS 910W) and is seen here at Aberdeen in the company's livery. The new ECW body style was soon to be seen in all corners of the NBC empire including the south and west regions. (Donald MacRae)

Bournemouth was an early convert to the new Leyland Olympian ONXB/1R and had its examples fitted with rare double-deck Marshall 78-seat bodies. Seen when still quite new at Southsea is No. 182 (TJT 182X), which had been delivered in January 1982 and was the 133rd chassis to be built; they were purchased to replace the PDR1/1 Leyland Atlanteans. (John Senior)

The Atlantean bustle disappeared on the new Olympian and a two-piece hinged engine door was fitted, supported by gas struts, greatly improving the appearance of the rear of the bus bodywork. Access to the sides of the engine compartment was by two doors, and under trays were also fitted. (Leyland)

Down in the west, Devon General took the Leyland Olympian into its fleet in 1983 and No. 1811 (A683 KDV) was one of the last chassis to be built at Bristol. These were ONLXB/IR type models with ECW 77-seat bodies. (David Toy)

The new Leyland Olympian began to appear with the fleets in the south and west, and the first Olympian for London Country was LR1 (TPD 101X), delivered in 1982 and fitted with a Leyland TL11 engine and a Roe 72-seat body. (David Toy)

Boro'line's expansion into contracts in London meant that it had to invest heavily into new buses, one of which is seen here. Delivered in 1988 it is number 759 (E159 OMD), a Leyland Olympian ON6LXB/1RH with Optare 76-seat body, working the contracted route number 132. The Optare company was formed from a management buyout from Leyland of the former Chas H Roe company of Leeds. (David Toy collection)

This London Olympian, L263 (VLT 9) but originally registered D263 FUL, was the final body to be produced at Eastern Coach Works before production was transferred to Workington and the Lowestoft factory was closed. It was the final chapter in the long-running dispute concerning the change from traditional craft-based coachbuilding to engineered-assembly (regarded as Meccano construction) which had already brought about the closure of Park Royal Vehicles in north London and taken out the AEC plant at Windmill Lane in the associated backlash. (Peter Durham)

7 : The Roaring Eighties

The Leyland Passenger Division was renamed with a slick title of Leyland Bus in March 1981. They were now standing as a separate identity and had their own sales and design team. The Olympian was selling alongside the Atlantean (which had gained large export orders) but sales were not as high as they could have been. London Transport had put their Daimler Fleetline DMS class up for sale through Ensign Bus. Many companies took the opportunity to purchase the second-hand Fleetline instead of new vehicles. This included the NBC companies of Maidstone and District, Hants and Dorset, City of Oxford, Western National and municipal Brighton Borough Transport. Further away West Midlands PTE had taken large numbers. It had been very rare for large companies to purchase second hand double-deckers but these Fleetlines were only six to eight years old and an opportunity not to be missed. With this number of second-hand vehicles on the market it depressed the requirement for new double-deckers.

By the early 1980s the majority of the PDR1 Atlanteans had been removed from service by NBC companies. Devon General's Atlanteans would be all gone by July 1984, Plymouth, Brighton and Maidstone and District were also removing the Atlantean in some cases PDR1A/1 and early AN68s. Southampton City Transport in 1982 had a 100% fleet of Atlanteans in their refurbished Portswood depot. In the early 1980s it would seem that the Atlantean was going to disappear from a large number of fleets as the new generation of double-deckers entered service and second-hand Daimler Fleetlines from London were also available.

The Leyland Atlantean production for the home market came to an end in 1984 and the Olympian was then Leyland's only double-deck chassis.

Maidstone and District had started a commuter express service to London and as passenger growth increased, they re-seated three Leyland Atlantean PDR1A/1

Portsmouth turned to East Lancashire Coachbuilders at Blackburn for their last Atlanteans in 1980. Operating on service 12 is Portsmouth's No. 345 (CPO 345W), one of the last ten Leyland Atlanteans for the city. (David Toy collection)

When Eastbourne required further double-deckers it purchased four from Ipswich Borough Transport in 1980. Dating from 1968 No. 64 (LDX 74G), a Leyland Atlantean PDR1/1 with the 74-seat full height version of the standard Eastern Coach Works body is parked in the depot.
(David Toy collection)

It's all going green; the Devon General fleet was being repainted into Western National's colours. Once proud in the old Devon General red and cream, No. 534 (NDV 534G) is a 1968 Leyland Atlantean PDR1/1 (O.680 engine) with an MCW 75-seat body which looks very plain in green. (David Toy)

In 1986 Plymouth changed its livery, adding black below the lower deck window line. This East Lancashire Coachbuilders-bodied Leyland Atlantean AN68B/1R, No. 148 (ATK 148W), dating from 1980, shows the new style. The East Lancs Atlanteans were to be the last in service with a major fleet in the south and west when they were withdrawn in 2006. (David Toy)

Portsmouth went back to a small number of Mk II Leyland Nationals in 1980, and all three had 40 dual-purpose seats. Parked at the Southsea Bus Rally is No.100 (CPO 100W) in the revised livery that was applied to the DP Nationals. (David Toy)

Southdown later moved to the Leyland National Mk2, and delivered in 1981 was No. 135 (RUF 435X), with 49-seats and room for 24 standing. This was one of the last batch of Nationals taken by Southdown.
(Southdown Enthusiasts club)

Brighton turned to single-deckers and purchased seven Leyland Nationals with Gardner 6HLXB engines. These vehicles were some of the last Nationals to be built, being delivered in 1983. Number 28 (XFG 28Y) is seen opposite the Brighton Pavilion. Brighton stayed with single-deckers and went on to purchase twelve Leyland Lynx between 1988 and 1990.
(David Toy)

Centre: London Country stayed with the standard NBC PRV/Roe body for its Leyland Atlanteans. Delivered in January 1981 is AN259 (KPJ 259W), a Leeds product, an AN68B/1R working a Crawley local service. When the last one was delivered a year later they had purchased 293 Atlanteans. (David Toy collection)

Above: In the early 1980s Maidstone & District had Leyland Atlanteans in service, and they were nearly 20 years old. Dating from 1963 No. 5610 (610 UKM) was a PDR1/1 with a Weymann body, seating 77, and still looking as if it could spend many more years in service. (M&D and East Kent Bus Club)

Bottom left: Delivered in 1981, its last year of production, is Southdown No. 268 (JWV 268W) a Bristol VRT/SL3/680 with an ECW 74-seat body. Seen in Brighton's Pool Valley bus station it is waiting for passengers for the Brighton to Portsmouth limited stop service which previously had been operated by Southdown's Leyland Atlanteans. This batch had Leyland O.680 engines fitted, due to the problems in obtaining engines from Gardner, who were experiencing industrial action. (David Toy)

Bottom right: An early purchaser of ex-London DMS class Daimler Fleetlines was Brighton Borough Transport which had two. Looking better than in its original dull all-over red is former DMS558, now No. 92 (MLK 558L) in the Brighton fleet. Its sister vehicle No. 91 was used as a permanent driver trainer. (David Toy collection)

Above: London Country operated the *Round London Sightseeing Tour* for London Transport and painted vehicles into London Transport Red. This picture shows Leyland Atlantean PDR1A/1R Special AN116 (MPJ 216L) which was used on this service. (David Toy)

Left: In 1983 NBC set up London Crusader for tours in London in competition with London Transport. Numbers AN10/11 were painted into Crusader livery. With not many passengers is AN10 (JPL 110K) a Leyland Atlantean PDR1A/1 Special with a 72-seat Park Royal body. (David Toy)

Foot: Due to the increase in passenger loading for its London commuter service Maidstone & District fitted coach seats and a higher ratio angle drive to three of its Leyland Atlantean PDR1A/1 Specials. In the black Invictaway livery is No. 5718 (FKM 718L), dating from 1973 and now fitted with 69 coach seats. (David Toy)

Facing page, centre right: Another London Country-operated *Round London Sightseeing Tour* vehicle in London Transport Red. This picture shows AN106 (MPJ 206L), one of two that were converted to a permanent open top configuration. (David Toy)

Facing page, foot: Another conversion at Southampton was No. 139 (WOW 529J), a 1971 PDR1A/1 Atlantean with East Lancs body which was turned into a permanent open top bus in March 1984 and renumbered 900. (David Toy collection)

Right: To upgrade its open-top fleet Eastbourne converted two former Ipswich Leyland Atlanteans in 1987. With few passengers on board No. 66 (LDX 76G) is about to return to Eastbourne town centre and still looks smart for a vehicle that is 13 years old. (Colin Routh)

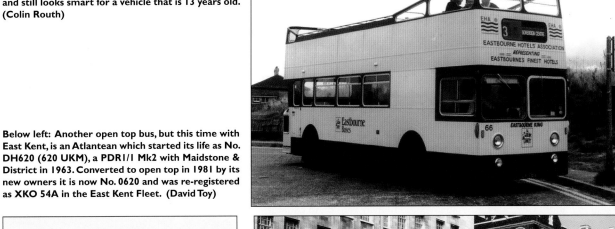

Below left: Another open top bus, but this time with East Kent, is an Atlantean which started its life as No. DH620 (620 UKM), a PDR1/1 Mk2 with Maidstone & District in 1963. Converted to open top in 1981 by its new owners it is now No. 0620 and was re-registered as XKO 54A in the East Kent Fleet. (David Toy)

specials with MCW bodies to coach seating. They were liveried in black and marketed under the Invictaway name.

London Country moved over to the Leyland Olympian after taking 293 Leyland Atlanteans and most municipal operators were purchasing small numbers of the next generation vehicles. With the end of the Bristol VRT production NBC turned to the Olympian as its standard double-decker.

Events started to happen in 1984 when the Greater London Council lost control of London Transport and London Regional Transport was set up. The latter would also be responsible for the tendering of London Bus Services.

Further away in Devon an experiment was being carried out using minibuses as a lower cost operation to the big bus. In time, many companies would follow this type of operation and remove further double-deckers from their fleets. Not all passengers were going to like this new cramped method of transport especially if they had buggies and children. Older passengers found the minibus difficult with restricted luggage space when shopping. By the end of 1986, there were over 750 minibuses in the fleets of companies in the south and west. In some cases, this had led to a complete change of policy on vehicle purchase. Devon General had over 230 and Plymouth City Bus had also invested heavily with 81 in its fleet.

The government produced the Buses White Paper on Transport in July 1984, which contained much radical thinking for the bus industry. The National Bus Company was to be split into smaller units and then sold; municipal bus companies were to be an arms length company of the local authority. Full deregulation of bus services was to be introduced except for London. In the south and west several of the well known NBC companies would be split up. Later in the 1980s this would include Maidstone & District which would lose its Sussex operation to a new company called Hastings and District. London Country would be split into four; Southdown would also be split into smaller units. Western National was also reduced into smaller operating companies including, Southern National, Devon General and North Devon. In the south central area Hants & Dorset was also split into two with a new Wilts & Dorset company.

Many of the early Leyland Atlanteans that were sold went for further service in other bus companies in the UK. Others were exported abroad to Hong Kong

With interest in double-deck coaches growing Leyland produced a chassis for an ECW coach body. Maidstone & District and London Country both took batches, the former for the Invictaway London services. They had Leyland TL11 engines rated at 245bhp, and 73 coach seats. Looking very clean is M&D No. 5444 (GKE 444Y) in the company's Invictaway livery. (David Toy)

and Australia where they went on for several years of further service. With the demise of certification by the Department of Transport in most cases there were no major body overhauls on buses. The decision to remove a vehicle could be due to the cost of maintaining the steel-framed bodies in conjunction with the start of minibus operation. Early Leyland Atlanteans were not always reliable vehicles and this was another reason for their removal.

There was a need in some areas to increase double-deck operation and when London Country won tenders in London it turned to the second-hand market for Leyland Atlanteans. Vehicles purchased from Strathclyde PTE brought the Alexander body into the double-deck fleet. Others came from Southdown and Northern General with the standard Park Royal/Roe NBC body. East Kent had purchased minibuses but needed more one-person operated double-deckers and also purchased the same style of Atlantean for its operation.

The first NBC company to be sold was Devon General on the 19th August 1986 and from then on, others followed them into private hands. In the same year, on the 26th October, deregulation of bus services was introduced. In some areas bus wars started and more vehicles were required and second-hand Leyland Atlanteans were to join some of the privatised fleets in the eighties. In several areas smaller independent operators entered service bus operation. Competition appeared where it was not expected in places like Bournemouth, Maidstone, and Medway Towns. The larger companies went into a defensive mode to protect their services.

Plymouth turned to the minibus in a big way starting with four in 1985, and then in the following year taking eighty. They were all Dodge 56 series with Reeve Burgess bodies. The majority had seating for 23, a vast difference from the Atlanteans that they had replaced. With an all-over advertisement livery for a carpet company No. 6 (D106 LTA) is parked in Plymouth's depot. (David Toy)

Things to come: Devon General went to a minibus fleet using Ford Transits with 16 seats, and continued this into privatisation when there would only be one conventional bus left in the fleet. An early purchase was No. 22 (A268 MTA), new in 1984 with a Carlyle conversion body. (David Toy)

8 : Deregulation and Privatisation

NBC in the South and West

By mid 1988 all the National Bus Companies had been sold and vehicles began to appear in their new company liveries. Hampshire Bus had gone to a new group called Stagecoach and further away in the west another new group was forming called Badgerline. Competition started with the newly formed companies in Bournemouth, Wilts and Dorset against the local authority fleet. Southampton City was also under pressure from competition from a new company called Solent Blueline whose parent was Southern Vectis on the Isle of Wight. In Maidstone a new operator By-Gone buses started competition with Boro'line (ex-Maidstone Corporation) and this started to put pressure on the company. With its spread into London contracts and heavy investments the reduction of revenue in the home town was taking affect.

Many of the new companies began to purchase new buses but there was still room for the Leyland Atlantean. Although production had ceased in 1984 for the home market earlier models of the AN68s were becoming available and several companies purchased them to help with their double-deck requirements.

COMPANY	BOUGHT BY	DATE	FLEET
Devon General	Management	19/08/1986	400
Southern Vectis	Management	07/10/1986	130
Maidstone and District	Management	07/11/1986	300
East Kent	Management	05/03/1987	320
Hampshire Bus	Skipborn/Stagecoach	02/04/1987	247
Provincial	Employees	08/05/1987	90
Brighton and Hove	Management	08/05/1987	220
Wilts and Dorset	Management	24/06/1987	210
Western National	Plymouth Coaches/Badgerline	06/08/1987	300
Southdown	Management	02/10/1987	320
Hastings and District	Management	16/12/1987	100
London and Country (South West)	Drawlane	19/02/1988	415
Kentish Bus	Proudmutual (Northumbria M.S.)	15/03/1988	168
North Devon and Southern National	Management	29/03/1988	300

When London Country Buses was split into four, new liveries were introduced which added colour to the scene. The South East company became Kentish Bus Company Ltd, reflecting better the area of operation. Kentish Bus went for a maroon and cream layout. This Leyland Atlantean AN68A/1R with a Roe body was new in 1980 as AN222 (EPH 222V) with its original owner. (David Toy collection)

London Country South West became London & Country in 1989, adding 'Limited' in 1992. They introduced this more colourful livery. AN223 (EPH 223V) shows off the new style working on the London contracted 65 service. (David Toy collection)

End of Portsmouth City Transport

Portsmouth had been a loyal Leyland customer with the Leyland PD1, PD2, PD3 and then as an early user of the Atlantean. By 1980 it had purchased over 150 Atlanteans, the last being ten with East Lancs bodies. There had been no investment in vehicles for five years, the last being three Dennis Lancets with Wadham Stringer bodies. With deregulation of bus services in October 1986 Portsmouth was about to be targeted by its next-door municipal operator Southampton. With the company now at arms length to the council, a new logo was used on the fleet at Portsmouth. Portsmouth's General Manager had proposed a management/employee buyout for the bus fleet, but this was rejected by the council in the later part of 1987. Southampton CityBus was forming a new company called Red Admiral with the Badgerline group to operate a minibus service in Portsmouth. This came into operation on 11th December 1987 with route A (Portsea to Pauls Grove). The council offered Portsmouth for sale, which made it even more vulnerable to competition.

Bids were invited and Southern Vectis became the preferred bidder but it was decided to allow a second round in order for the employees to place their own bid. For the second time Southern Vectis was the preferred bidder and it was agreed by the Secretary of State on the 3rd June 1986 that the sale could proceed. In the months leading up to this agreement the financial situation at Portsmouth was deteriorating due to the added competition. Southern Vectis announced that there would be redundancies and wanted to franchise out some of the routes to other operators. The council stated that this was not part of the terms of the sale and Southern Vectis withdrew their bid.

Portsmouth was eventually sold on the 26th October 1986 to a joint bid by Southampton Citybus (75% of the shares) and the employees of Portsmouth. The new name became Portsmouth CityBus with a new livery. Badgerline sold its shares in Red Admiral to Southampton CityBus.

The saga of Portsmouth CityBus was not yet over. Stagecoach Holdings purchased the company in 1989 but was investigated by the Monopolies and Mergers Commission. The Commission approved the takeover after investigating competition within the area. This was overruled by the Secretary of State for Trade and Industry and Stagecoach was ordered to divest itself of the company. Stagecoach sold the company to Transit Holdings in 1991. With its large fleet of minibus operation in the south west Transit Holdings was about to change Portsmouth into the same type of operation and the Atlantean would disappear from the fleet.

Showing the new Portsmouth logo is Leyland Atlantean AN68/1R No. 266 (VTP 266L) with an Alexander body. (David Toy collection)

The new livery of Portsmouth CityBus is shown on No. 343 (YBK 343V), a Leyland Atlantean AN68A/1R with an Alexander body. The fleet colours were not unlike that of their new owners, Southampton CityBus. (David Toy collection)

Also showing the Portsmouth livery change is East Lancs-bodied Atlantean No. 351 (CPO 351W). (David Toy collection)

Southampton converted two early Leyland Atlanteans to carry wheelchairs, the facility being advertised as Wheels on Wheels. Converted in 1985, No. 134 (TTR 168H) could carry four wheelchairs and 62 passengers, the capacity was later changed to six wheelchairs. A lift was fitted at the entrance. (David Toy collection)

The Portsmouth operation followed the Thames Transit norm by becoming a minibus operation. Blue Admiral Ford Transit 797 (D797 NDV), a Mellor 16-seat conversion is the new order for Portsmouth services, a change for the passengers after being used to large capacity Leyland Atlanteans. (David Toy collection)

In yet another livery is No. 287 (XTP 287L), a former Portsmouth City Leyland AN68/1R Atlantean with Alexander body which was one of the few double-deckers to be operated by Blue Admiral in Portsmouth. (David Toy collection)

In the short-lived livery of Stagecoach is ex-Portsmouth 342 (YBK 342V), a 1980 Leyland Atlantean with Alexander body. New owners were to be Thames Transit who turned the operation into a minibus fleet. (Southdown Enthusiasts Club)

Who Owns Leyland?

With the privatisation of the National Bus Company orders for new buses and coaches were falling at a dramatic rate and this was affecting Leyland sales. The government wanted to sell British Leyland, it had lost around £80m between 1982 and 1984. It had closed the Bristol factory and moved the Leyland Olympian production to Workington. The body plants of Park Royal and Eastern Coach Works had also to be closed. Further redundancies were taking place in other areas of Leyland Bus.

The 1986 orders from the shrinking National Bus were for only 133 Tigers and 41 Olympians. The Olympian production was moved again this time to the Farington works at Leyland. General Motors had made an offer for part of the empire including the truck division but not the buses. MCW wanted the bus division and inspected the Workington plant.

To counteract the bid the Leyland Bus Board gave permission for a management buyout bid for the company. Time dragged on with a falling market and eventually Leyland was sold to a Management team on the 13th January 1987.

The Leyland Olympian was to be offered with a Cummins L10 engine and ZF or Voith transmission. The Gardner engine would still be an option but demand was falling. Leyland's own troublesome hydracyclic gearbox could now die in peace. In the single-deck market, Leyland had replaced the National with the Lynx, which was taking orders very slowly. Who would have thought that the respected Gardner engine range was now in decline and by 1994 it would be no more. It had always been a busman's engine giving good fuel consumption and reliability. The new generation engines had to meet the forthcoming EURO1 regulations and Gardner would need a new engine to meet this. The management ownership of Leyland only lasted a short while and it was sold to Volvo on the 28th March 1988. It would not be long before the Leyland name would disappear from the product market.

For further information about this period and the demise of the once great Leyland company read *'Beyond Reality – Leyland Bus the Twilight Years'* by Doug Jack (Venture Publications).

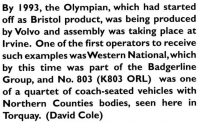

By 1993, the Olympian, which had started off as Bristol product, was being produced by Volvo and assembly was taking place at Irvine. One of the first operators to receive such examples was Western National, which by this time was part of the Badgerline Group, and No. 803 (K803 ORL) was one of a quartet of coach-seated vehicles with Northern Counties bodies, seen here in Torquay. (David Cole)

9 : Coming to the end of the Atlantean era

In London, London and Country hired 24 South Yorkshire Leyland Atlanteans for the London tendered services 78 and 176 until their new Volvo D10M East Lancs buses arrived.

Other operators were changing to minibus operation to save labour costs, Plymouth, after being a large Leyland Atlantean user and trying the Leyland National, turned to the Dodge 56 in a big way and by the end of 1992 the minibuses had grown to 60% of the fleet.

Brighton was also removing Leyland Atlanteans from its fleet in favour of single-deckers and Dodge 56 minibuses. The first East Lancs batch Nos.53-62 and Nos.63-4 from the second had all been sold by 1988; nine had travelled to Scotland to the fleet of Rennies of Dunfermline.

Southampton had steadily removed early Atlanteans from its fleet but with those remaining, they decided on a different strategy with an in-house refurbishment of its double-deckers. The Atlanteans were re-trimmed, the heating updated and the body had an overhaul. They also re-bodied five 1974 Leyland Atlantean AN68/1R chassis with East Lancs single-deck bodies with seating for 35 during 1991. To improve the ride the road springs had a revised setting, when compared to the new Dennis Dart with the same number of seats they were a heavy bus.

Southdown had been purchased by its management team in October 1987 and had a joint operation with Eastbourne buses under the Top Line brand for a short while. The name of Southdown was soon to disappear when the Management team sold the company to the Stagecoach Group on the 16th August 1989. Hastings and District was soon to follow and the Stagecoach livery was becoming a common sight within the South East.

Originating in the north east were eleven Leyland Atlanteans from Northern General with Park Royal bodies; these became London Country AN346-56. They were required for contracted London Regional Transport services, as indicated by the white panel on the front of the bus. (David Toy collection)

Southampton City Buses Portsmouth operation was sold to Stagecoach Holdings in October 1989. Large numbers of the Portsmouth Leyland Atlanteans were sold. Stagecoach was growing within the south.

In 1988 a new single-deck midibus entered the market; it was to become the new single-decker for most fleets over the coming years. The Dennis Dart with a Cummins B6 5.9litre engine fitted at the rear and an Allison transmission was to take the industry by storm. This was the beginning of the end for the large bus engine; the Cummins B6 could produce the same output as an 11.3litre Leyland engine of the past. The Dart moved into fleets and in some cases reduced the double-deckers even further.

For the story behind the transformation of London Transport's Country services (green buses) to NBC and subsequent division into four companies prior to that privatisation read *'London Buses 1985-1995'* by Tom McLachlan (Venture Publications).

Further vehicles arrived after the London Country operation was split into four parts. New in 1974, **AN380 (HJA 115N)** is a former Greater Manchester PTE Leyland Atlantean AN68/1R with a Northern Counties 75-seat body, now with London Country South West which subsequently became London & Country.
(David Toy collection)

With the winning of London Transport tenders, London Country required further double-deckers and it turned to a sister NBC company for eight vehicles. Not far from home is **AN304 (SCD 728N)**, a Leyland Atlantean AN68/1R with Park Royal body which came from Southdown, having being new in 1974.
(David Toy collection)

Maidstone Fails & More Privatisation

Maidstone Boro'Line had gone too far with its London operation. It had stretched it to a level it could not sustain and had large debts on new vehicles. Second-hand Leyland Atlanteans from Nottingham City had also been purchased to help with its services. It had gained London tenders with disastrous financial results, and in 1991 it was offered for sale by the council owners. Maidstone had competition within its home ground with Bygone and Turners buses and also its big brother Maidstone and District. To protect its interest within the town Maidstone and District introduced services over the top of Boro'Lines Maidstone operation. Boro'Line started operations within the Medway towns with ex-Nottingham Leyland Atlanteans but this was short lived and the company went into administration in April 1992, the London operation was sold to Kentish Bus which included 57 vehicles. This left Boro'Line with 61 vehicles, it all came to an end on the 29th May when Maidstone and District purchased 43 of the vehicles and the head office at Armstrong Road.

In 1993, both the Southampton and Brighton municipals were sold to their employees and in the same year, the management at East Kent sold their company to the Stagecoach Group.

The operation of the Leyland Atlantean was far from over. Second-hand vehicles were being purchased by both large and small operators. Maidstone and District, who had purchased Atlanteans from GM Buses, turned to Luton and District for a further supply, they had the standard NBC Roe or Park Royal body. Eastbourne was also purchasing second-hand examples from various operators to speed up one-person operation. Southampton purchased Park Royal-bodied Atlanteans from Plymouth during 1993. In January 1994, the Management of Brighton and Hove sold the company to the Go-Ahead group and later that year had borrowed two Leyland Atlanteans from Tynemouth and District, these were purchased after a few months in service.

The two British Bus-owned companies within the area, Kentish Bus and London and Country, still operated a large number of ex-London Country Atlanteans. Many of these were refurbished by London and Country and had a new seat trim.

Boro'line purchased twelve Leyland Lynx for its 108 (Lewisham to Wanstead) London Transport contract. The buses were based at Greenwich and at one time there were more buses operating on London contracts than in the home town of Maidstone. Delivered in 1991, No. 816 (H816 EKJ) was a 49-seat Gardner-engined Lynx. (David Toy)

Maidstone Boro'line won a London tender for route 188, Euston-Greenwich, and needed buses to operate the service until its new vehicles arrived. Leyland Atlanteans from Ipswich Transport were hired in to cover. Working on the 188 is Ipswich No. 87 (WPV 87L), a Leyland Atlantean AN68/1R with Roe 72-seat dual door body new in March 1973. (David Toy collection)

Below: Maidstone Boro'line also hired buses from Kingston upon Hull City Transport to help cover its London contracts until new vehicles arrived. Working the 328 service is No. 378 (WAG 378X) a Leyland Atlantean AN68C/1R with Roe 74-seat body new in 1982. (David Toy collection)

Manufacturing Developments

On the manufacturing front Volvo announced that production of the Olympian was to be moved to the Irvine plant in Scotland. The Olympian would now be a Volvo product with the Volvo TD102KF engine as standard, the only option would be the Cummins L10. After a long association with the bus industry going back to the 1930s the Gardner engine was no longer available to the industry. Other items on the chassis were changed to Volvo manufacture. The Cummins option did not last and with Euro2 only a Volvo engine was offered.

Dennis introduced a new rear-engined double-decker called the Lance; this was later changed to the Arrow. It had an inline Cummins C-series engine with ZF transmission. London and Country needed to replace its Leyland Atlanteans and Nationals and ordered ten Arrows and the last four Dennis Dominators to be built. They went on to purchase large numbers of low floor Dennis Darts, which removed the majority of the Atlanteans over the coming years.

To remove further Atlanteans Brighton Blue Bus ordered 15 low-floor Dennis Darts for delivery in 1996. Next-door Eastbourne had become a customer of DAF for both single- and double-deckers reducing again the Atlantean. Southampton still had a large fleet of Leyland Atlanteans and the Dennis Dart was also purchased to make inroads into the removal of the once favoured chassis.

Maidstone and District was sold to British Bus on the 18th April 1995 and two months later First was born between the merger of GRT Holdings and Badgerline.

Kentish Bus, who still had ex-London Country Atlanteans, painted them into a new livery of green and yellow for buses that were used on their commercial services. Competition appeared on the south coast when Leisurelink operated a service between Brighton and Newhaven and used an ex-Seadog open-top Leyland Atlantean that once belonged to Devon General.

Over the next three years changes took place that removed the majority of the Leyland Atlanteans from the south and west companies. Obtaining spare parts was becoming more difficult and life on the main components was reduced due to the number of times they had been overhauled. Good quality core items for the Leyland

The first Dennis Darts had Carlyle Dartline bodies, entering service with London Buses in 1990. Given fleet No. DT49 (G47 TGW) was an 8.5 metre long example with 28 seats. The new Dennis Dart replaced a large number of double-deckers in the south and west over the forthcoming years. Plaxton was to produce a more attractive body styling for the Dart that became very popular. (David Toy collection)

O.680 engine (cylinder blocks and heads) were also becoming difficult to find. Cowie purchased British Bus on the 1st August 1996. Plymouth announced that its remaining Atlanteans would not be used for front line services, but only on schools and contracts work. In May 1997, Brighton Blue Bus was sold to Brighton Hove and District and 12 Atlanteans were within the sale. A small number were repainted into the new owners' livery and by the following March all were withdrawn. Not long after on the 1st August Southampton Citybus was sold to First. The large ex-London Country fleet of Leyland Atlanteans had all gone by the end of the decade. Dennis announced its new low-floor double-deck chassis in 1998, which was to become the Trident and in the same year the Volvo B7 range was also announced. In the south-west one of the few ex-NBC independents, Southern National/Devon Red Bus, still had three ex-Blackpool East Lancs-bodied Leyland Atlanteans.

At the turn of the century, there were two main operators of the Leyland Atlantean, First Southampton and Plymouth Citybus. Southampton purchased a number of MCW Metrobuses in order to remove the Atlantean but due to their inflexibility they were kept on schools duties. The Atlantean worked alongside the new Volvo B7R artic and B7 double-deckers in all day service. By 2002, the fleet was down to 14 and many had body structural problems due to the road calming on the Southampton routes. The end came on the 5th February 2005, when the last Atlantean No.38270 (FTR 270X) was removed from service at Southampton. They were replaced by Dennis Arrows from the First London fleet.

The end came to the Leyland Atlantean when Plymouth removed its No.171 (TTT 171X) a 1981 AN68C/1R with an East Lancs body on the 15th October 2006 after the company had operated the Leyland Atlantean for 46 years. Plymouth was the last of the original purchasers of the Atlantean in the south and west and it must be a record that will be hard to beat on operating a vehicle type for this length of time.

Brighton Blue Buses was sold to Go-Ahead subsidiary Brighton Hove & District on the 20th May 1997 and included were twelve of the Atlanteans. They had a short life with their new owners and only three of them were fully painted into Brighton & Hove livery. Now numbered 804 (TYJ 4S) with its new owners and fully re-liveried, it only lasted until February 1998 before it was sold. (David Toy)

New Leyland Atlantean Deliveries

Fleet No.	Reg. No	Chassis Type	Body	Date in Service
Maidstone and District				
DH490-523	490-523 DKT	PDR1/1	Metro-Cammell H78F	1959
DH524-525	524-525 DKT	PDR1/1	Metro-Cammell CH60F (Interior finished by Weymann	1959
DL43-56	43-56 DKT	PDR1/1	Weymann L53F	1959
DH526-50	526-50 HKJ			
DH551-70	551-70 LKP	PDR1/1	Metro-Cammell H77F	1960-61
DH571-585	571-585 RKJ			
DH586-632	586-632 UKM	PDR1/1 Mk2	Weymann H77F	1962-63
5701-5720	FKM 701-720L	PDR1A/1R Special	Metro-Cammell H78F	1972-73
Devon General				
DL872-888	872-888 ATA	PDR1/1	Metro-Cammell H78F	1959
DL895-917	895-917 DTT	PDR1/1	Roe H75F	1960
DL918-24	918-24 GTA	PDR1/1	Roe H75F	1961
DL925-33	925-33 GTA	PDR1/1	Metro-Cammell CO75F	1961
526-31	EOD 526-31D	PDR1/1 Mk2	Willowbrook H75F	1966
532-541	NDV 532-541G	PDR1/1 Mk2	MCW H75F	1968
London Country				
AN1-90	JPL 101-190K	PDR1A/1 Special	Park Royal H72D	1972
AN91-120	MPJ 191-220L	PDR1A/1 Special	Metro-Cammell H72D	1972-3
AN121-123	VPB 121-123M	AN68/1R	Park Royal H72D	1974
AN124-147	UPK 124-147S	AN68A/1R	Park Royal H73F	1978
AN148-158	VPA 148-158S			
AN159-183	XPG 159-183T	AN68A/1R	Park Royal H73F	1978-79
AN184-202	XPG 184-202T	AN68A/1R	Roe H73F	1979
AN203-232	EPH 203-232V	AN68A/1R	Roe H73F	1979-80
AN233-237	JPE 233-237V	AN68B/1R	Roe H73F	1980
AN238-292	KPJ 238-292W	AN68B/1R	Roe H73F	1980-81
AN293	MPG 293W	AN68C/1R	Roe H73F	1981
Southdown				
701-714	PUF 131-144M	AN68/1R	Park Royal H73F	1974
715-727	PUF 715-727M			
728-737	SCD 728-737N			
738-741	SUF 138-141N			
742-747	LCD 42-47P	AN68/1R	Roe H73F	1975
East Kent				
7001-7015	JJG 1-15P	AN68/1R	ECW H74F	1976

Fleet No.	Reg. No	Chassis Type	Body	Date in Service
London Transport				
XA1-37	CUV 1-37C	PDR1/1 Mk2	Park Royal H72F	1965-66
XA38-50	JLA 38-50D			
Plymouth Corporation-Plymouth Citybus				
121-138	TCO 521-538	PDR1/1	Metro-Cammell H77F	1960
139	UDR 339	PDR1/1	Metro-Cammell H77F	1961
140-148	VDR 940-948	PDR1/1	Metro-Cammell H77F	1961
149-160	WJY 749-760	PDR1/1	Metro-Cammell H77F	1962
161-183	YCO 261-283	PDR1/1	Metro-Cammell H77F	1963
184-191	BDR 184-191B	PDR1/1 Mk2	Metro-Cammell H77F	1964
192-198/200-202	DDR 192-198/200-202C	PDR1/1 Mk2	Metro-Cammell H77F	1965-66
199/203-205	DDR 199/203-205D			
206-220	FJY 906-920E	PDR1/1 Mk2	Metro-Cammell H75F	1967
221	JJY 221G	PDR2/1	Park Royal H77D	1968
222-244	JJY 622-644G	PDR2/1	Park Royal H79D	1969
245-263	MCO 245-263H	PDR2/1	Park Royal H77D	1970
1-15	NDR 501-515J	PDR2/1	Park Royal H77D	1971
76-90	GDR 201-215N	AN68/1R	Park Royal H72D	1975
91-105	LTK 91-105R	AN68A/1R	Roe H72D	1977
106-120	OCO 106-120S	AN68A/1R	Roe H72D	1978
121-135	STK 121-135T	AN68A/1R	Roe H72F	1979
136-147	VJY 136-147V	AN68A/1R	138/143 East Lancs. H75F 139-142/44-47 East Lancs. H71D	1979/80
148-157/160-161	ATK 148-157W/160-161W	AN68B/1R	East Lancs. H71D	1980
158-159	ODV 203-203W	AN68B/1R	East Lancs. H71D	1981
162-171	TTT 162-171X	AN68C/1R	East Lancs. H74F	1981
Portsmouth City				
201-225	201-225 BTP	PDR1/1	Metro-Cammell H76F	1963
226-235	226-235 CRV			
236-245	BBK 236-245B	PDR1/1 Mk2	Metro-Cammell H76F	1964
246-254	ERV 246-254D	PDR1/1 Mk2	MCW H76F	1966
188-189	RTP 188-189J	PDR2/1	Seddon B40D	1971/2
190-199	TBK 190-199K			
255-272	VTP 255-272L	AN68/1R	Alexander H75D	1972
273-293	XTP 273-293L	AN68/1R	Alexander H75D	1973
294-301	GOT 294-301N	AN68/1R	Alexander H75D	1975
302-319	HOR 302-319N			
320-334	UOR 320-334T	AN68A/1R	Alexander H73D	1979
335-344	YBK 335-344V			
345-354	CPO 345-354W	AN68A/1R	East Lancs. H73D	1980
Bournemouth Corporation				
170-179	AEL 170-179B	PDR1/1 Mk2	Weymann H74F	1964
200-219	HEL 200-219D	PDR1/1 Mk2	Weymann H74F	1966
220-236	ORU 220-236G	PDR1A/1	Alexander H74F	1969
240-249	SEL 240-249H	PDR1A/1	Alexander H74F	1969/70
250-265	ULJ 250-265J	PDR1A/1	Alexander H74F	1970/71
270-285	XRU 270-285K	PDR1A/1	Alexander H74F	1972

Fleet No.	Reg. No	Chassis Type	Body	Date in Service
Maidstone Corporation				
27-34	EKP 227-34C	PDR1/1 Mk2	Massey H74F	1965
35-42	JKE 335-342E	PDR1/1 Mk2	Massey H74F	1967
43	NKK 243F			
44	OKJ 844F	PDR1/1 Mk2	Massey H74F	1968
45-46	OKM 145-146G			
47-50	AKE 147-150K	PDR1A/1	Northern Counties H74F	1971
51-54	EKR 151-154L	AN68/1R	Northern Counties H74F	1972
Southampton City				
101-104	OCR 145-148G			
105	OCR 149F	PDR1/1	East Lancs. H76F	1968.
106-120	OCR 150-164G			
121-122	TTR 155-156H	PDR1A1/1	East Lancs. H76F	1969/70
124-136	TTR 158-170H			
137-161	WOW 527-551J	PDR1A/1	East Lancs. H76F	1971
162-171	EOW 395-404L	AN68/1R	East Lancs. H76F	1972
172-186	PCR 295-309M	AN68/1R	East Lancs. H76F	1974
187	JBK 886P			
188-94	HTR 558-564P	AN68A/1R	East Lancs. H76F	1975
195	HTR 557P			
196-201	HTR 565-570P			
202-216	MCR 202-216R			
217	ORV 90S	AN68A/1R	East Lancs. H76F	1977
218	MCR 218R			
219	ORV 89S			
220-231	PPB 220-231S	AN68A/1R	East Lancs. H76F	1978
232-246	UPO 232-246T	AN68A/1R	East Lancs. H76F	1979
247-261	YRV 247-261V	AN68A/1R	East Lancs. H76F	1980
262-266	DBK 262-266W	AN68A/1R	East Lancs. H76F	1981
267-271	FTR 267-271X	AN68C/1R	East Lancs. H76F	1981
272-276	KOW 272-276Y	AN68C/1R	East Lancs. H76F	1982
Brighton Corporation				
81-85	TUF 81-85J	PDR1A/1	Willowbrook H73D	1971
86-90	WUF 986-990K	PDR1A/1	Willowbrook H73D	1972
43-52	CUF 143-152L	AN68/1R	Willowbrook H73D	1973
53-62	JFG 353-362N	AN68/1R	East Lancs. H73D	1975
63-72	OYJ 63-72R	AN68A/1R	East Lancs. H73D	1977
1-15	TYJ 1-15S	AN68A/1R	East Lancs. H74F	1978
Eastbourne Corporation				
11-17	KHC 811-817K	PDR1A/1	East Lancs. H76F	1972
18-25	GHC 518-525N	AN68/1R	East Lancs. H75F	1975
26-27	RHC 726-727S	AN68A/1R	East Lancs. H74F	1978
28-31	VDY 528-531T	AN68A/2R	East Lancs. H82F	1978/9
32-35	YJK 532-535V			
36-37	CJK 36-37V	AN68B/1R	East Lancs. H74F	1980

Fleet No.	Reg. No	Chassis Type	Body	Date in Service
Silver Star				
35	TMW 853	PDR1/1	Weymann L73F	1959
37	VAM 944	PDR1/1	Weymann L73F	1960
40	XMW 706	PDR1/1	Weymann CL61F	1961
42	1013 MW	PDR1/1	Weymann L73F	1962
BOAC				
	LYF 304-318D	PDR1/1 Mk2	Metro-Cammell CH54F	1966
	GML 846-851J	PDR2/1	Roe CH65F	1971
Chisnell Winchester				
	HOR 589-592E	PDR1/2	Roe H77F	1967
Halls Hounslow				
	VYH 46-48G	PDR2/1	Roe H68F	1969
	LLH 5-9K	PDR2/1	Roe H69F	1972
Note: What would have been Southampton 123 was destroyed in the fire at East Lancashire Coachbuilders in 1970.				

Although the Atlantean has passed from every-day service, examples can still be seen at rallies and other events. Here, the former Southdown No. 731 (SCD 731N), a Park Royal-bodied example, poses for the photographers at the Dunsfold airfield, site of the Cobham Rally in April 2011. (John Senior)

Acknowledgements

I could not have written this book without the help of many people and enthusiasts' groups as well as reference to various publications including some very early editions that go back in time. Special thanks go to the help from Brian Weeden of the M&D and East Kent bus club for providing me with advice and the supply of photographs. Jack Parsons who worked for Silver Star, many years ago, helped with information and photographs on the company, Colin Curtis for the help with photographs of the FRM and his experience of the Atlantean in London. The Southdown Enthusiasts' Club who allowed me to use their photograph collection. Harry Postlethwaite, who in the early days gave me many ideas and advice. Two other people are John Senior and Bob Rowe of Venture Publications who put the book together and supplied additional photographs. David and Mary Shaw, Venture's proof readers, are also thanked for their patience and attention to detail.

Reference was made from various articles in magazines, manufacturers' brochures and books including Buses Illustrated, Buses, Bus & Coach Magazine, Passenger Transport Magazine. Reference was made to various other books including The Leyland Bus (Doug Jack), Leyland Atlantean (Ron Phillips), Devon General (Leslie Folkard), Southdown (Collin Morris), Ian Allan ABC British Bus Fleets of various years, Major Bus Operators (Nicholas King), Capital Bus Handbooks, again various years, and The PSV circle chassis lists on the Leyland Atlantean. My last thanks must go to my wife Barbara who has been by my side throughout my career in the industry and encouraged me to write this book after I retired.

On Reflection

The Leyland Atlantean served the south and west for 47 years and after its early problems became a much respected bus – it even ended up on London contracts in the 1990s. There are various examples now in preservation spanning the vehicle's history from the early production, (Devon General, Maidstone and District) to later types (London Country, Brighton, Southampton, and Portsmouth Corporations). These can be seen at various rallies around the country where enthusiasts and others can see the simplicity of its engineering when compared to the modern bus of today.

With today's legislation, bus design is changing each year. We have seen the Dennis Trident, Volvo B7 and now we have the Enviro 400 and Volvo B9 ranges. I do not think that we shall ever see a production run as long as the Leyland Atlantean with a bus that changed very little to its original design. There can be no other tribute to the Leyland Atlantean than its own statistics; there were over 15,000 Atlantean chassis built and 12,000 of these for UK operators; of this 57% were in the AN68 series. The figures speak for themselves.

Not long to retirement: number 1263 (DBK 263W) a Leyland Atlantean AN68A/1R with East Lancashire 76-seat body by this time owned by First Hampshire & Dorset waits for its next turn of duty in Southampton City centre. These former Southampton Atlanteans could still be seen on all-day service right up to the end. The bus was delivered in 1981 and withdrawn in 2004, giving 23 years service to the passengers of the City. The last Atlantean was withdrawn on 5th February 2005. (David Toy)